The Public Service
and
University Education

EDITED BY

Joseph E. McLean

1949

PRINCETON UNIVERSITY PRESS

PRINCETON, NEW JERSEY

PRINTED IN THE UNITED STATES OF AMERICA
BY PRINCETON UNIVERSITY PRESS AT PRINCETON, NEW JERSEY

CONTENTS

Contents

THE PUBLIC SERVICE
AND UNIVERSITY EDUCATION

INTRODUCTION

BY JOSEPH E. MCLEAN

"YOUNG MAN, won't you learn a lesson in the primer of politics that it is a *prima facie* evidence of littleness to hold office under our form of government? Great men get into office sometimes, but what this country needs is men that will do what we tell them to do. . . . If the great men in America took our offices, we would change to an empire in the next ten years."[1] Such was a theme of an itinerant preacher of the 1890's, who, in his favorite sermon, *Acres of Diamonds*, extolled the virtues of money-making and, conversely, condemned the idea of public service. A generation after the McKinley era, an acute observer, Charles Merriam, noted that, with the exception of the first generation of our national existence, "American public life has suffered severely from the lack of a tradition of public service on the part of men of wealth and leisure." In the intervening years, however, great crises—internal and external—have dramatized the challenge of public service and have attracted able men and women—including some of wealth and leisure—to government service.

This challenge of public service has quickened with the expanding role of government. The federal government's assumption during the past decade and a half of a more positive role in the domestic economy and the current tentative beginnings of international government have thrust unprecedented burdens upon those who administer the public's business. Government personnel has become a paramount consideration in the increasingly important administrative process, which is today

---

[1] Richard H. Conwell, *Acres of Diamonds* (New York, 1915), pp. 50-51.

concerned not merely with the execution but also with the formulation of public policies. In terms of courage and character, of training and experience, the public servants of to-morrow—particularly those in executive positions—must be broader gauged and better equipped than were their predecessors.

The ever-pressing need for responsible and responsive government means that the public service can and should compete with business and the professions for its fair share of the talented men and women of America. That need has been given increasing recognition in the past few years.

Not that the *Acres of Diamonds* theme has been completely discredited. The terms *bureaucrat* and *politician,* in too many quarters, connote fumbling, inefficient third-rate individuals with a tenacious hold on the public purse. And the blame for a variety of society's ills is passed on to the "government" by a public that all too frequently fails to discriminate between governmental and nongovernmental factors or between politicians and career civil servants.

Fortunately, for the many-faceted theme of this volume, all of its contributors, at one time or another, might properly have been labeled *bureaucrats.* And to confound those who hold to a rather rigid definition of that label, some have actually met pay rolls. Some of these authors are professional, or career, public servants; others, amateurs, drawn from private enterprise or the academic world. Regardless of their amateur or professional standing, however, they are all motivated by a strong personal sense of responsibility for the public problems that must be solved if the American life-way, in its private and public aspects, is to continue.

All of these contributors were active participants in the Princeton Bicentennial Conference on University Education and the Public Service.[2] The challenging atmosphere of that

[2] November 13-14, 1946. A summary of the conference was published by the Princeton University Press in January, 1947.

Introduction

conference and the significance of the issues there debated suggested the potential values of this symposium. In view, both of the recent crisis experience and of the magnitude of the current and future tasks of government, it was felt that this volume might contribute to that stream of knowledge that had for a generation been replenished by such conferences as the Minnesota and Princeton conferences of 1931 and 1935, by such basic studies as those of the Commission of Inquiry on Public Service Personnel, and by such individual studies as George Graham's *Education for Public Administration*.

This volume, of course, is not intended to be a definitive study of personnel training and management. If anything, in Rowland Egger's words, it is directed "to basic issues of social and governmental organization, to social and administrative values, and to intellectual and moral convictions about the shape of things to come" and is "related primarily to the larger and more fundamental problems of the relationship between higher education and the public service in a free society." Although it is not definitive, this book in its basic plan is intended to be comprehensive in scope. We are interested in the personnel needs of government in both the domestic and foreign realms. We are interested in the experience of our British colleagues. And we are interested in the capacity of American universities to meet certain expressed needs of government.

In the several essays of this symposium, there is inevitably a certain degree of overlapping, not only necessary, but wholesome as well. Several of the authors, amateur as well as professional, comment upon the growth and complexity of governmental functions. And, although there is a section devoted to the British experience, many of the contributors are not immune to the fascination of indulging in comparisons and contrasts of the British and American experiences. These necessary overlappings and the tendencies of both the practical men of affairs and the academicians to offer counsel to each other do not detract from the main thesis of this volume; rather they reflect, and indeed add to, the integrating forces that are making governmental and academic institutions sensitive to their mutually supporting roles.

Implicit in the plan of this symposium is the assumption that the policies and practices of government and the universities are interrelated. Indeed, the essays are intended: first, to assay the personnel needs of government; and, second, to examine the role of the university in the education of prospective public servants.

These objectives are entwined in the several parts and essays of the symposium. In the first part, Patterson French draws particularly upon his experience in the Office of Price Administration and in the Bureau of the Budget to discuss the wartime personnel experience of federal agencies. Mr. French's non-Civil Service Commission point of view is then followed by the views of Civil Service Commissioner Arthur Flemming. Disagreeing on minor points, both men agree on the need for decentralization of personnel activities and for a closer liaison between government and the universities.

In the second part of the symposium, three eminently qualified administrators present a top management view of the federal service. One of them, Donald C. Stone, is a professional public administrator, who now occupies a key position as Director of Administration of the Economic Cooperation Administration. The other two writers are, in a sense, amateurs, who are possessed, however, of a great breadth of experience in public and private activities. Robert A. Lovett, now Undersecretary of State, served as Assistant Secretary of War for Air during World War II. These experiences supplement his activities as a partner in Brown Brothers Harriman & Co. and he is eminently qualified to approach the problems of government from the point of view of a business executive. H. Struve Hensel is a New York lawyer who served the public interest as

Introduction

Director of the Legal Procurement Division and as Assistant Secretary of the Navy during the war; in the course of his official duties, he had occasion to observe British civil servants in action and hence, in his discussion of problems of structure and personnel, is able to contrast British and American practices.

The third part of this volume sets aside the international field for particular consideration. Two of the writers in this area are career diplomats. Seldon Chapin, now Minister to Bulgaria, was Director of the State Department's Office of Foreign Service during the significant period when the Foreign Service Act of 1946 went into effect. George F. Kennan, after twenty years in the field, is now directing planning activities in the State Department. He is especially qualified to speak on both the character and training needs of the foreign service. The third writer in this field is Frederick S. Dunn, who may be labeled an academician since he is Director of the Yale Institute of International Studies and previously taught at Johns Hopkins University. But blended with his academic experience is a wide-ranging series of special and very practical assignments in the official conduct of our foreign relations. And it is significant that he places great stress on the decision-making process as the core of our general conduct of international relations.

Although the British experience is a thread that runs through many of the essays, a separate section of this volume was set aside to focus attention on past and current developments in the British civil and foreign services. One of the writers, Sir James Grigg, rose to the top rung of the British administrative ladder and, uniquely, was appointed a minister while serving as a civil servant. As Secretary of State for War in Prime Minister Churchill's cabinet and more recently as alternate director of the International Bank for Reconstruction and Development, Sir James speaks authoritatively on all aspects of the British civil service. The second British representative in this volume, E. L. Woodward, Professor of Modern History at Oxford University, is an academician who has had practical wartime experience in the British foreign service and who brings to bear a detached point of view. The third writer in this section of the symposium is an American, Paul Appleby, Dean of the Maxwell School of Citizenship and Public Affairs at Syracuse University. In the course of a decade and a half of government service, Dean Appleby held such responsible positions as Undersecretary of Agriculture and Assistant Director of the Bureau of the Budget and, in addition, participated in several international conferences. In his brief, pungent essay, he basically questions some of the traditional views that we and the British have held about the British civil service. It is fair to say, at this point, that he raises these questions on the basis of an examination of the papers submitted by Sir James Grigg and Professor Woodward and that space does not permit a rebuttal on the part of the two able British writers.

The final section of the symposium is devoted to the mutually supporting roles of government and higher education in the United States. Professor John Gaus, of Harvard University, discusses a university-wide approach to the problem of educating men and women for the various civil services in a complicated social setting. Professor Rowland Egger courageously tackles the issue of whether or not there can be an American administrative class and, in a refreshing manner, considers some of our traditional viewpoints on this matter. Both of these writers are educators who from time to time have served the public in various capacities at the state and local, as well as federal, level of government. The third and final essay, "Managing the Public's Business," is the work of an able executive who since 1940 has been continuously in the public service. During that time as Undersecretary and then as Secretary of the Navy, and now as Secretary of Defense, James Forrestal has displayed an intense interest in the many problems of public management and in the particular prob-

Introduction

lem of attracting able men and women to the public service. It is fitting that the concluding essay in this volume should be the work of a hard-hitting executive who has had both public and private experience and who has evidenced a positive interest in the role that may be played by the universities.

No good purpose would be served by attempting a comprehensive synthesis of the views expressed by the contributors to this volume. It may be pertinent, however, to point out both the major areas of agreement and the issues that cannot be resolved in this series of essays.

First, and it is an obvious first, there is a general awareness of the changing role of government and of the environment in which public servants must work. This observation applies equally to both the domestic and foreign areas in which government now operates. Mr. Chapin speaks of the "new diplomacy . . . the power of public opinion . . . relations between peoples rather than between governments" and calls for something more than "the rituals of old school-tie diplomacy." The business of the foreign service has changed in character, covering a much wider field, largely owing to the immense increase in the functions of government. The intrusion of complicated economics into politics necessitates an understanding on the part of foreign service officials of the economic structure of the modern world, as well as an ability to discern interests outside the circles of diplomatic capitals.

The foreign service is, of course, not the sole branch of the public service that has experienced recent changes in function and environment. Federal, state, and local governments generally have assumed new functions or expanded the old; and considerable recognition has been accorded the personnel problem particularly since 1930. Indeed, as Professor Gaus observes, we have come to recognize, instead of a single vocational entity dubbed "the public service," a great variety of public services covering such categories as department heads, the

Introduction

workers in substantive fields, and the more recently defined
auxiliary service and general staff personnel.

In considering one particular personnel category—top management—Mr. Stone includes both administrative and general
staff positions—"the heads of departments and agencies and
their principal operating and staff assistants, and similar officials in the bureaus and other major subdivisions within departments. They are persons whose functions are almost entirely managerial or administrative, in contrast to 'technical.'
Their energies are devoted broadly speaking to defining the
objectives of their agencies, planning the program, developing
an organization properly staffed to carry out the program,
scheduling and budgeting the program, developing the necessary interrelationships, channels of communications, work
habits, and doctrine for the organization to move forward as
a harmonious team, establishing devices for control and coordination, exercising oversight and guiding the operations
of the establishment, and maintaining and reacting to many
external relationships."

These public managers operate in an environment conditioned first of all by the relation of a democratic government
to the people. Mr. Lovett observes that whereas our system of
government stood the critical test of world-wide conflict, documented testimony has revealed the inefficiency of German governmental management. "Ruthlessness did not prove to be a
substitute for responsibility to the public." The public accountability of government executives frequently results in
healthy criticism; in some cases, however, the criticism may be
irresponsible and destructive. As Mr. Lovett notes, some able
men avoid government service, the main deterring factor being
"fear on the part of the individual that, no matter how blameless he is, he may be used as a target to get headlines by some
sensation-seeking politician."

In addition to external pressures, Mr. Stone remarks on the
internal resistances—passive and overt—that may complicate

the life of a public manager. Unreconciled differences, specialists asserting particular interests, the deadening effect of routine, incompetence or disloyalty—any or all of these may block the teamwork so essential to a successful organization. Managerial authority, he observes, is not a push-button affair, and cannot operate on a command basis. Indeed, top management is frequently the prisoner of the organization and must use leadership, persuasion, and cooperative effort.

The complexities and wide-ranging activities of government impress both the career public servant and the relative newcomer. Mr. Lovett is quick to point to the dangers of oversimplification. Noting the lack in many businessmen of an adequate appreciation of public administration, he suggests two major needs today: "(1) a wider understanding of the problems of government by businessmen; and (2) the desirability of working out some sort of triple interchange of personnel between business and government, between the universities and government, and between business and the universities."

It was to be expected that the recent emergency experience would reveal critical personnel deficiencies in the federal service. Mr. French, for example, singles out three kinds of people who were in scarce supply and whose scarcity should be a matter of concern in the years ahead: "people with perspective and insight into the nature of the governmental process; leaders without biases; and people who know how to run an organization." More particularly, he concludes that we tend to overemphasize, in peace as well as in war, the specialized nature of the work done in government by economists, lawyers, political scientists, sociologists, and other social scientists.

Along similar lines, Mr. Lovett refers to a "phenomenon in the federal service—the surprisingly large number of specialists, technicians, and experts in government." This overemphasis on the specialist contributed to underemphasis on the generalist and trained manager. "The latter were in relatively scarce supply. I say 'relatively scarce' because there were, scattered throughout government agencies, a number of extremely competent public administrators. But they were harder to find than specialists." The specialists receive additional criticism from Mr. Stone, who observes that the specialist may tend to oversimplify the problems of government and may produce dogmatism and prejudice; he must, when dealing with other than purely technical considerations, come to understand something about the social-political-economic-environment within which his particular responsibilities are carried out.

The need for men drawn from a more general experience is also noted by Mr. Forrestal, who states that sometimes people with specialized training "tend to rely too much on the techniques of their training to the detriment of practical solutions." And Professor Egger, after commenting on the alarming wartime deficiency in the administrative group, as well as the postwar exodus of many good administrators, predicts that the European Recovery Program will probably recapitulate the administrative errors of the past decade and a half. "This is one of the minor costs of not having an administrative class with a well-established and generally accepted role in federal top-management."

To correct these critical personnel deficiencies and in general to attract more able young men into the public service involves a modification of government policies. Certain changes are already in the making; additional changes are suggested, ranging from increasing salaries to the creation of a permanent undersecretary in each federal department.

Among the significant wartime developments in personnel administration was the decentralization of the Civil Service Commission's activities. Mr. French notes approvingly a trend toward an improvement in the status of agency personnel offices; Mr. Flemming reports a postwar extension of the wartime policy of decentralized recruitment, involving the co-operation of top operating officials as well as outstanding sub-ject-matter specialists. The decentralization program holds implications for colleges and universities and should spur co-operation between federal officials in the field and university authorities.

Part of the solution to the over-all problem of improving the public service involves improving the service's public rela-tions. Ignorance about the service is appalling. To raise the prestige of the service Mr. Flemming, for example, suggests higher salaries in the higher grade levels; opportunities for continued training; new programs for promoting career serv-ants; and less emphasis on literal enforcement of regulations. He further suggests that the universities and colleges help by developing in their students at least an elementary knowledge of government as well as acquainting them with opportunities in the service.

One of the additional suggestions made for improving the public service involves a structural change in an endeavor to provide greater administrative continuity in the higher levels of federal agencies. Mr. Forrestal draws upon his experience in the Navy Department as evidence of the need of a permanent undersecretary or assistant secretary "who could provide the politically appointed department head with a background of knowledge so that when it is called upon to face substantial expansion there is at least a small cadre of trained people to provide the advice and guidance which any newcomer to gov-ernment will need."

In other areas, of course, governmental policies are having an impact. In the international field, the federal government has only recently undertaken a drastic reorganization of the foreign service. Prior to World War II, certain obstacles, real or apparent, had stood in the way of attracting able young candidates for the service (such as the absence of opportunity for specialized talents and the idea that an independent income was the prime requisite for a career). The urgent needs of the new diplomacy, reports Mr. Chapin, were behind the reorganization of the service as provided for in the Act of 1946 which, besides increasing pay and allowances, provided for three branches of the service: *line* (the permanent professional service), *staff* (roughly equivalent to the former administrative, fiscal and clerical services), and *reserve* (officers available for special temporary service). In addition, a new Foreign Service Institute has been established to provide various types of training for the three branches and to direct college liaison. It is significant that about half of the officers will follow a program of area specialization, while others will follow the "generalist" line.

Much remains to be done by government if it is to meet its share of the responsibility for providing the conditions under which a democratic career service may be developed and under which our democratic system may be preserved. The universities, also, share in this over-all responsibility. Mr. Lovett, for example, directs the attention of our educators and leaders "toward the creation of a tradition of individual responsibility among all of us. . . . What is really needed, in my opinion, is far greater emphasis in our educational system as a whole and especially in our universities, on the preparation of students for responsible citizenship, both *inside* and *outside* government." And Dr. Dunn, in his challenging essay on "Education and Foreign Affairs," concludes: "Today's greatest danger is perhaps the overwhelming pressure for a resolution of the current two-power conflict by some dramatic action, such as a Soviet-American war. Only if advances are made on the three levels of understanding of research, university instruction, and adult education will this danger be eliminated. For then a responsible decision-maker backed up by an enlightened and patient public opinion can make an unspectacular series of

Introduction

small (but correct) decisions instead of a single dramatic (but possibly categorically wrong) big decision."

In the more particular area of curriculum, the views of the contributors to the symposium are more divergent. The most significant issue is probably that of the "social sciences versus the humanities" in the spelling out of a broad liberal education. The importance of a broad general training is a keynote of Mr. Forrestal's essay. Pointing out that the French and Germans have relied largely upon specialized education, he concludes: "The British have relied upon broad cultural and scientific training, designed to give men power of independent thought, ability for clear and lucid expression of ideas and, possibly the most important of all, what may be called the humanistic attitude that government shall remain the servant, and not become the master, of the people.

"I believe the broad general training is preferable."

Numerous observations—whether they concern training for the public service generally or training for a particular branch —turn on an answer to the basic question: What is a liberal education?

"To have a liberal education it is not enough to know 'the trees, the birds, the bees,' and to be familiar with good books, great plays, and immortal poetry. Nor is it sufficient to have knowledge and appreciation of music, painting, sculpture, and architecture. It is also necessary to know something of social, economic, and political institutions. We can no longer take the social order for granted."[3] And, added Professor Graham, "Systematic introduction to the social sciences is particularly important for the prospective administrator."

These views of a social scientist may be contrasted with the following remarks by Sir James Grigg, an advocate of humanistic education, who states that he is "not a believer in the value of the law or economics faculties as a training for the general administrative part of the public service. . . . I do not

[3] George Graham, *Education for Public Administration* (1941), p. 113.

15 ·

believe in institutes or faculties or theoretical courses of public administration. . . . I am convinced that the art of managing men cannot be imparted in schools or university courses or public lectures." Sir James' views are bound to provoke sharp disagreement. Indeed, they run counter to the trend in Britain, as reflected in the recent changes in the administrative examination system that increased materially the weightage for law and economics. ("For my part I regard nearly all these changes as retrograde. It certainly increased the encouragement to specialize, it tended to diminish the encouragement to a humanitarian education, and it attracted more and more of the students who gave their main attention to law and economics.")

A middle-ground position is taken by Professor Woodward, who notes two schools of thought: "One school inclines to push vocational training back into the university years and to encourage specialization in the social sciences. The other school holds that our business is not necessarily to give men an introduction to the practical matters with which they will have to deal later on but to provide them with the best kind of mental background and training." He observes that it has been true in the past that a classical training has supplied the English administrative services with candidates of high excellence. It does not follow, however, that "other disciplines are not capable of producing results as good or better. . . . In any case, whether we think it a good or bad thing, the position in England now is that, except for a minority, the classical discipline cannot be made a *sine qua non* because it requires a long grinding at school, and this preliminary work at Latin and Greek is unlikely to be possible at the average state school which does not possess the necessary staff."

With respect to the new subjects, however, he feels that at present they are not very satisfactory; the problem is how to make them into a vehicle for general education. In the process of adjusting courses at Oxford, he personally saw an attempt to recover something that would give the undergraduate *a sense of form*. Urging that we should install French into the place once occupied by Latin in our educational system and admitting his uneasiness about the second rateness of so many of our works on contemporary politics and economics, he emphasizes his view that a civil servant "should learn at the university to see men as the great masters have seen them."

A different note is struck by Mr. Appleby, who questions the idea that the best mental training can come from education that has nothing to do with the problems of today—political, economic, and social. Similarly, Dr. Dunn argues, "Surely there can be no special virtue in irrelevance of subject matter as such." And Professor Egger, drawing upon personal experience, offers an engineering course dealing with the history of sewage disposal in ancient and medieval times as the one university course that for him opened up vistas of humanistic knowledge.

The "social science" philosophy is evident throughout Professor Gaus's remarks, whether they concern the responsibilities of universities or the professional training in the undergraduate years. As to the former, he states: "Those responsibilities include the fostering of a greater awareness among all the constituent schools of the public aspects of their fields and of specific recruitment opportunities; participation in counseling or advisory services; formulation of curriculum and course provisions whereby the ecology of government and the role of the processes of government are made integral parts of the basic general education of all students; and continuing encouragement of programs at all levels of government whereby methods of recruitment and training will better facilitate our governments in obtaining and making use of the products of our educational institutions."

Finally, Professor Egger, after considering the qualities that we may seek in the generalist and drawing upon the reports of the Commission of Inquiry on Public Service Personnel (1935)

Introduction

and of the President's Committee on Civil Service Improvement (1941), reasons that even if the art of managing men cannot be imparted by formal instructional methods, the principles and practices involved in the scientific use of the tools of management can be taught. He also concludes that an American administrative career service can be established, one that would be compatible with our tradition of equality of opportunity and one that would involve no de-emphasis of professional education, which is a special characteristic of American education.

Taken together, the essays seem to point to the following essential conclusions:

(1) There is a critical lack in the federal service of men with those qualities usually associated with the higher grades of the British civil service, men who have breadth of experience, maturity of personality, and a capacity to deal with large matters of state.

(2) There is currently no program to develop such men, nor are there well-established posts at the top of the American public service for career men of these qualities. The responsibility for developing such a program rests with the highest levels of government.

(3) Any plan that may be developed by government cannot be a pale imitation or mere importation of the British administrative system. We must devise a system (a) that will be in harmony with American traditions, (b) that will aim at high levels of intellectual and personal capacity, (c) that will put an emphasis upon the production of generalists, and (d) that will feature adaptability rather than rigidity.

In his contribution to this volume, Dr. Dunn has occasion to say: "The fields of education and public affairs share these things in common, that they are basically important to the adjustment of man to his world, and that they readily inspire misty thinking and melodious platitudes. When the two fields

Introduction

are united in a single discourse, there is an obvious risk of leaving behind an impressive trail of ponderous trivialities." Needless to say, in the editor's view, the obvious risk has been run and the result is impressive evidence of hardheaded, rather than misty, thinking.The broad areas of agreement and disagreement, reflected in these essays, are significant for citizens in and out of government, or in and out of the universities, who realize that a democratic public service characterized by ability and vitality is essential if man and his civilization are to survive.

PART I

WARTIME PERSONNEL EXPERIENCE

WARTIME PERSONNEL ADMINISTRATION IN FEDERAL AGENCIES

BY PATTERSON H. FRENCH

ONE WHO tries to think back over our wartime experience in public administration is likely to have two contrasting reactions in rather rapid succession. At first he feels that the war must have crowded a lifetime of experience into a few short years; that we must have made discoveries in the field of management similar to atomic fission or the miracles of medicine. When he tries to be more specific about these advances, however, he begins to feel that the period may have been so completely one of crisis, dislocation, and improvisation that it can teach us nothing.

The real answer is probably a more humdrum one. The war brought no spectacular administrative advance, but it left us with a clearer recognition of many challenging administrative problems and with a rich mine of recorded materials for those who want to dig into them. One of the exceedingly important tasks of the next few years, and one to which universities can contribute significantly, is the analysis of this wartime experience to learn—as quickly as possible because we need the answers now—what lessons these six years of supreme administrative effort hold for us.

This last war was an extremely well-documented one, to the extent of some nine to ten million cubic feet of papers. It was marked by the most systematic attempt in our governmental history to record and analyze wartime administration while the war was still going on. Under the auspices of a Committee on Records of War Administration composed of leaders in the social sciences, over forty federal agencies established historical staffs that will leave behind them very substantial contributions to future knowledge in the form of administrative histories, special studies, and collections of important agency papers.

The field of wartime personnel is unusually rich in research possibilities but the important studies have yet to be made. Some of the historical units in federal agencies have produced special reports on their own personnel activities, but these are only beginnings. Thorough work, broad in scope and penetrating in method, on government-wide personnel problems and practices is still in the future. We need research by many people—working not necessarily under single supervision but certainly in some kind of harmony—on many subjects in the area of our wartime personnel experience: personnel developments in the decade preceding the war; the effect of these developments on personnel administration during the war; the new personnel functions, problems, and needs created by the war; the sources of government manpower; the areas of critical personnel deficiencies; methods of recruitment and selection; personnel performance in relation to training and experience; organization for personnel management; the relative functions of the Civil Service Commission, agency personnel offices, and operating units; and the transition to peace, including—and this is an important factor—an analysis of the kinds of people who have left the government service and what has happened to those who have stayed.

In the absence of systematic research, some preliminary contribution has been made and can be made by people who have lived through the wartime experience in Washington and who may have found time for some reflection. This essay attempts such a contribution from the point of view of one who participated during most of the war period in the operation of emergency programs that were never easy and often very hectic. There is, of course, the risk that the point of view will be warped, since it was fashionable during that period for operating people to view personnel officers and other staff officials as bottlenecks if not as actual traitors. The view is tempered, however, by a period of postwar reflection and can be balanced against the views of personnel administrators and others who saw the picture in different, and perhaps superior, perspective.

At the risk of belaboring the obvious, something must be said about the setting against which wartime personnel administration took place. Federal civilian employment in the continental United States more than tripled from 1939 to its peak in the middle of 1943. More than two million jobs were created; the number of employees that had to be found, placed, and utilized must be multiplied by an unknown figure because of the exceedingly high rate of turnover. To illustrate the problem more concretely, the hundred days following Pearl Harbor saw the creation of the War Damage Corporation on December 13, the Board of Economic Warfare on December 17, the Office of Defense Transportation on December 18, the Office of Censorship on December 19, the Office of Production Management on January 7, the National War Labor Board on January 12, the Combined Raw Materials Board on January 26, the War Shipping Administration on February 7, the National Housing Agency on February 24, and the Office of Alien Property Custodian on March 11—ten major personnel operations in a little over three months.

Most of the work was completely novel. A little group of OPA employees, for instance, will always carry vivid memories of their emotions when they were first told that they were to issue 140 million ration books, a step that would commit the federal government to general consumer rationing for the first time in its history. Civilian defense was another completely new venture; we had never before felt a real threat to lives and safety at home. The list of pioneering activities is almost endless, from the development of a comprehensive industrial priority system to the regulation of the length and sweep, as well as the price of women's skirts.

The normal market for government personnel underwent drastic alteration. There was a constant flow outward from government as personnel enlisted, were drafted, or shifted to jobs in private industry. At the same time there was a flow inward toward government, consisting of people who patriotically wanted to get closer to the war effort; people whose former jobs had been hit by material shortages or other factors; and people who, because of the general tendency to pull up roots, were willing to try government service to see whether it might offer more pay, more status, more excitement, or simply a change. There was a marked feeling of impermanence in government positions themselves; large numbers of people worked for two, three, four, or more agencies during the war period. To the recruiting officer this last phenomenon was not a case of inflow or outflow, but rather of catching people as they went by, or robbing Peter in another agency to pay Paul in one's own organization.

The personnel practices and trends that developed against this background can be considered under four headings: the process of selection; training, experience, and performance on the job; critical personnel scarcities; and problems of the transition to peace. The subject is so large that each point will have to be handled in a very broad outline, principally to point out the areas that need more thorough study. To bring even a generalized discussion within manageable limits, attention will be given largely to personnel whose jobs required them to deal with problems of a general administrative, social, and economic nature—the kind of personnel that might be expected to come from educational backgrounds in the social sciences.

One of the major problems of war administration was simply that of finding people. The flow of people to government positions, mentioned earlier, was by no means automatic. People who would not have been available for government work before the war were often quite willing to participate if someone came to them with a description of useful public service to be performed. Often, those who volunteered had no specific assignment in mind but had to be matched up with the work that needed to be done.

As the war effort progressed, the center of emphasis in finding people to fill jobs shifted from the Civil Service Commission to the operating agencies. In general this shift took place more extensively at the higher grade-levels than at the lower. The commission located and placed large numbers of clerical employees, manual workers, and some other standardized kinds of personnel. In the intermediate levels, much of the burden was carried by agency personnel staffs and by the operating staffs. Recruitment of top executives was done, as a rule, by the operating officials most directly concerned.

The shift was inevitable. It came because the job of recruitment was greater than the commission could possibly handle. Operating officials, for the most part, pressed for direct control of their own recruitment; most of them had little or no previous experience with the complexities of government personnel procedures and almost all of them felt, rightly or wrongly, that they needed direct control over this important part of their work.

Coupled with changes in the methods of finding potential employees, a change occurred in the controls over the appointment of people when candidates had been found. At least from the point of view of the operating official, customary controls in the form of registers, certification, and the rule of three virtually disappeared during the war. The appointment papers might carry some technical language, generally unintelligible to the operating executive, referring to "selective certification" or something known as the "U-100" examination (a very broad, unassembled examination for general executive personnel), or some other specialized appointment device. Regardless of the technique—a matter of policy to the Civil Service Commission but of semantics to the operating man—the idea of picking an employee from a list of eligibles furnished by the commission was foreign to the experience of most wartime executives.

While administrators could thus go very far in hiring people of their own choosing without regard to formal examinations or the position of the candidate on an eligible list, candidates were required to meet certain standards that were maintained by the Civil Service Commission and by the agency personnel offices. In general, these standards were tied to the nature of the job and to the grade-level for which the candidate might be eligible. For instance, an applicant's record might qualify him for a position as a business analyst but not as an economist. He might qualify for the grade of CAF-12 (part of a series of symbols that constantly mystified administrators from the business world) but not for CAF-13; this represented a difference in pay and in organizational stature that was frequently a factor in the case of recruitment.

This basic approach, requiring candidates to measure up to standards of job-groups and grade-levels rather than requiring the supervisor to choose from the head of a line of candidates (or from the end if the line had moved up), has much to recommend it. During the war it was dictated by necessity; more elaborate methods would not have worked. An administrator could move flexibly in one of his most important functions, that of building a staff that could carry out his responsibility as he saw it. At the same time, machinery was provided for a certain amount of consistency and certain basic standards.

A system of this kind will work only if operating officials are generally conscientious. Our wartime experience was encouraging in this regard; there were surprisingly few cases in which bad appointments resulted from venal motives, outside pressures, or even personal favoritism. In peacetime the motivations of a supreme war effort are missing and the problem of preventing the misuse of the appointing power is more difficult. Yet we might well utilize our wartime experience to question the time-tested (or time-worn) method of the lineup, with its assumption that the commission can pick people wholesale better than the administrator can pick them for his individual needs.

Specifically, we might ask questions like these: are we possibly moving in the wrong direction by concentrating on the refinement of examining methods, especially in the case of administrative personnel? Can professional examiners, with or without the advice of operating people, evaluate with any nicety the relative merits of a group of applicants for jobs that require such qualities as judgment, imagination, and a flair for leadership? Can the relative order of candidates on, say, an eligible list for organization and methods examiner be equally acceptable to appointing officers in the Budget Bureau, the State Department and the War Assets Administration or can it be equally applicable for positions of staff technicians and supervisors?

In short, this is a good time to propose that we have reached a stage of administrative maturity when we can well put more emphasis on supporting the administrator who wants to do a good job and less on restrictions that might keep him from doing wrong and will certainly complicate his effort to do right. Of course, our opportunity to move in this direction depends somewhat on Congress, since legislation limits the area of action in this field. There are, however, a good many methods of skinning a cat if people want to skin one, and the Civil Service Commission can find procedural paths to move a considerable distance if it wants to. Efforts to locate good personnel, to improve the status and morale of the professional service, and to provide basic personnel standards are worth much more thought and research than intricate techniques for forming a queue at a bus stop when we are not even quite sure which bus will come along next.

One of the most useful results that could come from the

study of our war experience would be a neat set of conclusions, supported by reliable documentation, as to the kinds of training or experience that equip people to function successfully in given kinds of jobs. It is most unlikely, however, that the results of any such study would be either neat or conclusive.

Certain sources of personnel were drawn upon heavily and, on the whole, advantageously, during the war. For example, we entered the struggle with a very great advantage because of the large core of able and experienced government workers that had been developed in the federal service during the preceding period. The growth of government activities that began in 1933 attracted a group of competent, relatively young people, many of whom were ready when war came to assume important responsibilities in the emergency agencies. If agencies like WPA, PWA, and the Social Security Board had not existed earlier, our wartime personnel problems would have been much more difficult.

Another very substantial contribution was made by the universities through their contribution of staff members and of alumni with graduate training. In spite of the fashion of scoffing at professors, the academic group proved themselves to be surprisingly practical and adaptable. Graduate training in a number of fields demonstrated its practical value in the quality of the service rendered by students with advanced degrees, notably in economics, business administration, public administration, political science, and law.

The relation of business experience to effectiveness in government work is harder to evaluate and would be exceedingly difficult to study systematically. So many businessmen were drawn into government, from so many kinds of businesses, and for so many kinds of jobs, that endless examples could be marshaled to prove almost any point. Perhaps all that can be said here is that it would be difficult to prove either that businessmen are automatically equipped to be good government executives, or that businessmen are at a hopeless disadvantage because of their unfamiliarity with government procedures. Unquestionably, business contributed many strong and capable individuals; government ought to keep some of them and should, somehow, contrive to attract others like them.

One of the interesting phenomena of the war period was the limited extent to which people's work bore any relation to their education or experience. Any wartime administrator can give examples: a division in one of the war agencies dealing with commodity production and distribution was competently managed in succession by an economics professor, a political science professor, a retail drygoods merchant, and an automobile salesman. The same division had an economic analysis unit engaged in rather difficult problems of relating operations to business economics; unusually effective work was done in turn by a trade association consultant, an economist from an old-line government department, a business management engineer, an executive from a drug concern, and a junior executive from a garment manufacturing business who was wholly self-educated past the second year in high school.

Perhaps this war experience justifies the general conclusion that we should emphasize, in peace as well as in war, the broad and varied nature of the work done in government by economists, lawyers, political scientists, sociologists, and other social scientists. To take one example, emergency agencies such as WPB and OPA were liberally supplied with lawyers. A very small percentage of these lawyers wrote legal briefs or handled litigation. Most of their work was much more generalized; they drafted operating documents, participated in the formulation of the policies to be embodied in these documents, reviewed instructional and informational material, and dealt with many kinds of special petitions or appeals. Economists are another example; "economic analysis" involved many problems of policies, politics, and operations. The development of the "maximum average price" plan for clothing, for instance, under which a manufacturer could set his own pattern of production at various price levels so long as his total came within a given average price, involved all kinds of questions: how such a plan would affect the pattern of competition; whether it could be understood by the manufacturers; what elements of report- ing and control would have to be introduced to make it en- forceable; what exceptions would have to be made for special cases; and how it would fit in with other production controls imposed on the same people. The economist's most useful role was as a rather generalized planner and analyst, dealing with questions of whether a plan would work, how it would have to be administered to make it work, and what relation, if any, might exist between available statistical and economic facts and the actual impact of the plan if it were tried.

This emphasis on the combined specialist-generalist is likely to continue and it can serve as one of the foundations of a healthy and attractive career service. People of imagination, flexibility, and sound training will be attracted only to govern- ment careers that offer breadth and challenge. Government personnel practices that foster such careers and university teaching methods that develop the needed versatility can well combine to improve our career service.

It is difficult to comment on the kinds of jobs that were hard- est to fill during the war or on the kinds of trained personnel that proved to be most scarce in terms of the demand. It is im- possible to say, for instance, that good personnel technicians were scarcer than good statisticians or that competent informa- tion men were harder to find than competent administrative officers. If we approach the problem on a somewhat broader basis, however, we can single out three kinds of people who were in scarce supply and whose scarcity should be a matter of concern to those who are now planning higher education for the years ahead. These three are people with perspective and insight into the nature of the governmental process, leaders without biases, and people who know how to run an organization.

As to the first group, the point to be made is simple. People coming into government had, as a general rule, less ability to adapt their previous training or their particular specialties to the conditions of government activity than they should have had. This is said with full recognition of the novelty of the wartime tasks and the great difference between methods of operation in government and in private business.

One of the great educational experiences of the war resulted from throwing people from all kinds of former pursuits abruptly into government positions. These people usually expressed their first reactions in terms of the red tape to be encountered, the number of clearances required for every action, the lack of coordination within an agency and between agencies, the low quality of personnel (usually other people's personnel), and the lack of control of one's own operations. The more reflective of the newcomers gradually began, however, to appreciate the real differences between government activity and other kinds of enterprises.

One characteristic of government that is more often seen than understood is that it is inevitably and essentially a big enterprise. Many a division director found himself with a payroll of a half a million dollars a year (a fairly insignificant enterprise in the wartime governmental picture and not outstanding in size even in normal times); a business activity of the same size would be a rather substantial one. Mere bigness, wherever found, requires systematization, specialization, a recognition of the part played by other parts of the organization, and a reduced amount of freedom for lone wolf action.

A more important characteristic was the magnitude and complexity—the economic and social overtones—of the tasks that people, even in the lower ranks, were called on to perform. A manufacturer of shoes, experienced in deciding what kinds of shoes his company will make or what prices will be charged for them, has a very different job when he becomes a government official and prescribes the kinds of shoes that the whole industry can make or the prices that the industry can charge for them. The economist does his research, not because he plans to publish a book under his own name, but because he is participating in activities that may have immediate impact on people everywhere. The lawyer prepares an opinion, not because he is trying to win a case for one person or one company, but because he is helping to form policies that may affect the lives of many people.

One great need, that the universities can help to meet, is for people with greater understanding of government in the modern world—its purpose, its function, and its intimate relationship to the entire fabric of the nation's life. Intellectual grasp of this kind has been all too rare in recruits entering government. In the case of the businessman, for instance, wartime government work usually involved the major recasting of a deeply ingrained pattern of thought, based on a concept of separation between government and business that is no longer realistic. In the case of the lawyer, the economist, and other professionally trained personnel, the problem was to make a good generalist out of a good specialist. The function of the technical specialist-adviser, somewhat on a pedestal, which is at least implied in a great deal of our present professional training, does not fit the need for a flexible specialist-participant in practical government operations. For instance, to the extent that lawyers were not used as effectively in many wartime operations as they might have been, some of the difficulty can be traced back to the hesitancy of most law schools to recognize the importance of economic, social, and administrative considerations as an integral part of legal training. In the case of economists, the problem was one of insufficient familiarity with the managerial and operational implications of their economic thinking.

The case of people trained in political science, and particularly in public administration, was similar. These people, supposedly at least, have a grasp of the processes of public administration as a primary result of their training. Some question can be raised as to how effective that grasp proved to be in wartime situations. Among people trained specifically in public administration there was frequently a better grasp of the tools—budget formulation, personnel techniques, property management, and the like—than of the machinery that the tools can help to build. Political scientists, too, were very often less proficient than they should have been in using the concepts of economics and public law.

Thus, our war experience seems to have raised questions about the specialization—or compartmentalization, perhaps—of education as it has been practiced in the past. The goal is to achieve balance, to produce people who will be proficient in their specialties and at the same time see as clearly as possible how their specialties fit into the whole picture.

There are some signs that this problem is being recognized. Several universities are moving toward combined curricula in business and public administration. There is growing interest in courses that combine the approaches of several fields in the social sciences. A few forward-looking law schools are introducing subjects that would have raised a storm a generation ago; there is still a great deal of inertia, however, in taking the next step toward actual combination of some of the training in law schools with that in other professional schools.

We need to advance much further in the attack on this problem. We need much more than the fitting together of a jigsaw puzzle of pieces drawn from different departments. What is needed is the recognition that the study of public problems is at its core one study, where all the social sciences need to blend into a new adventure of thought and intellectual exploration toward a better grasp of the whole social picture.

Another central personnel deficiency during the war can be described as the need for leaders without biases. The war showed us that we had a scarcity of key leaders with a truly public point of view to fill our highest administrative posts. Most of the men with the needed administrative ability, energy, and mental capacity had been identified principally with particular interests; their representation of the national interest was largely coincidental.

The experience in the Office of Production Management is an excellent example; this had to be created as a two-headed establishment under Messrs. Knudsen and Hillman, to try to get a broad national point of view by the process of adding together more particularized points of view. This is no reflection on the honesty or impartiality of our wartime leaders. It simply means that major policy-forming jobs in the national government need people who are seasoned in dealing with public problems, and that the filling of this need provides a responsibility and a challenge to our entire educational system. Potential leaders need to be given perspective and an incentive to turn their best energies toward wrestling with public problems. Government itself needs to make a contribution, too, by improving its environment so that some of the people with capacity for leadership can look to government service as a worthwhile path to later leadership. Some help may come from the steadily growing interrelationship between public and private problems; as people recognize, no matter what their occupation may be, that their activities are increasingly of public concern, more attention may be paid to public activities and there may be more willingness on the part of superior people to participate in these activities.

The third area of scarcity is more earthy: it is the simple scarcity of people who have that sixth sense of how to run an organization. One reason is the obvious one; there were so many organizations to be run that it was necessary to make administrators out of college professors, salesmen, lawyers from one-man firms, and many others without any experience in this exacting pursuit. So much of the success of a good executive comes from qualities of personality and temperament that it is difficult to speak in terms of what the universities might do to aid in their production. Research on administrative ability might provide some guidance. Perhaps students of business management, public administration, and psychology might pool their efforts to give us more light. Probably government itself has much responsibility for providing opportunities for the development of such executive talent as they may find in its ranks as well as for making government service more attractive for people who have such talent.

As far as the government personnel service is concerned, the transition to peacetime operations has generally been one of facing so many immediate problems that very little could be done to build foundations for the future. The Civil Service Commission has a monumental problem in straightening out the federal service: regularizing the temporary war service status of many thousands of employees (and disposing of some, but not all, of the employees themselves); providing for the sudden surge of veterans who want to enter, or return to, the service; and correcting the inconsistencies and inequities that inevitably crept into our emergency operation. The agencies themselves are either liquidating, or reconverting to peacetime work, or, like the Veterans' Administration and the State Department, gearing themselves for new postwar tasks that are almost emergency operations in themselves.

In the course of this hurried, day-to-day business, much harm has been done in failing to create an atmosphere of career opportunities that would keep the more competent war service people in government posts. As a consequence, the group that has left the government may well be superior to those who remain. (This would be an interesting subject for a research project.) The need for a career service that will attract and keep good people has long had intellectual acceptance; we are unfortunately losing the greatest opportunity we have ever had to keep the good people in government while we have them there. Perhaps this could not be helped during the difficult reconversion period. It is a field, however, in which we cannot be proud of our postwar efforts, and it is a subject that needs to be taken more seriously in the future than ever before.

Many of the steps that need to be taken—and taken very promptly—to strengthen government service have been suggested earlier in this chapter. The government itself has a major responsibility: to do a better job in its personnel administration, to move away from the routinized mechanical concepts that block its view of the larger human problems, and to provide a kind of personnel utilization that will challenge people who are big enough to handle the big jobs that government has to do.

The colleges and universities also have two major responsibilities. They can provide the research and analysis—with independence and detached perspective—that is needed if we are to learn what we can from our experience. They can, and must, create for government a reservoir of capable and interested personnel, particularly of young people, who understand public problems and are eager to help in their solution. The need is there; the interest on the part of students is surely there. The manner of meeting the challenge is up to the colleges and universities.

3

THE ROLE OF THE UNITED STATES
CIVIL SERVICE COMMISSION

BY ARTHUR S. FLEMMING

PRIOR to World War II recruiting for the federal government
was a highly centralized operation. A considerable portion of
the workload involved was centralized in the Civil Service
Commission. As far as the commission was concerned, a large
part of the operation was centralized in Washington. Generally
speaking, there was a conviction, shared by persons both in and
out of government, that this was the only way in which a system of open competition could be effectively administered.

The reasons for such a belief were clear to all concerned.
The civil service system was brought into being in order to fight
a spoils system. A reluctant Congress brought it into existence
because of an insistent demand upon the part of the public;
and a hostile group of operating officials were determined to
prove that a merit system couldn't work. Consequently, sur-
rounded as they were on all sides by enemies of a merit system,
the first civil service commissioners decided that it was impera-
tive to keep a close check on the handling of each individual
case. Centralized controls, in their judgment, were absolutely
essential to the survivorship of anything resembling a merit
system. Unquestionably this nation is indebted to those who
held in a determined manner to such a concept. They are the
persons who are responsible for the deep roots which the merit
system now has in the federal government.

But with the advent of World War II, it began to appear that
centralization was not feasible. The reasons for this were obvious. Centralization resulted in delays. Delays of months and

even years in establishing lists of eligibles were cited in support
of this point of view. And many times, even after long delays,
it was felt that the best qualified and available personnel had
not been secured. Also, centralization of recruiting kept operating officials from playing an active role in the selection of
their personnel. In other words, centralization violated a basic
principle of sound management.

With the outbreak of war in Europe, many persons assumed
that it would be impossible for the federal government to utilize the civil service system in meeting its recruiting needs.
They assumed that speed in recruiting and an open competitive
system were irreconcilable. They assumed that active participation by operators in a recruiting program would likewise be
impossible within the civil service framework.

The Civil Service Commission did not accept these basic assumptions. It believed that it could spearhead a program which
could be carried out expeditiously. It also believed that it
could provide for active participation by operating officials in
recruiting activities. The commission asked for and received authority to issue special wartime regulations. (It was
specified, however, that persons appointed under the special
regulations should not receive a regular civil service status.) As
a result, over 7,000,000 placements were made in the federal
government during the war period under the general direction
of the Civil Service Commission. After the spring of 1940 no
one seriously proposed taking any of the wartime jobs out from
under the civil service system.

Consequently, it can be assumed that the wartime administration of the system at least did not stand in the way of the
total war program. In fact, there is ample evidence pointing to
the conclusion that the civil service system definitely facilitated
the wartime recruiting of civilian employees. Here in brief is
the role which the commission played throughout this period:

1. The commission determined minimum qualifications for
jobs.

2. The commission determined whether persons proposed for appointment met the qualification standards.

3. The commission participated actively with the departments and agencies in recruitment programs. There was a genuine pooling of resources.

4. The commission served as the War Manpower Commission's representative in regulating federal recruiting activities.

5. In the discharge of all of its recruiting responsibilities, the commission, in most instances, decided to maintain controls by (a) establishing standards; (b) delegating authority to act to the lowest possible operating level in its own organization, and to the departments and agencies; (c) ascertaining whether or not there was adherence to standards; and (d) taking corrective measures whenever it was determined that there was nonadherence to standards.

With the war over, the commission was faced with the necessity of determining to what extent it was going to continue its policy of decentralization, and to what extent it was going to return to a policy of centralized controls.

The decision has been made. And the effect of it is to carry decentralization even further than it was carried during the war. Though the decision applies to all aspects of personnel work, the discussion here will be confined to the field of recruitment. And here is how it is being carried out in the recruitment field:

1. The departments and agencies of the federal government have been invited to establish United States civil service boards of examiners within their departments.

2. These boards are to be made up primarily of top operating officials, and outstanding specialists in subject matter fields.

Nominations for membership on the boards must be approved by the Civil Service Commission.

3. The boards are to be established both in Washington and in the field service.

4. These boards are to develop, subject to the approval of the commission, minimum qualifications requirements for positions for which they hold examinations.

5. Also, these boards, in cooperation with the commission, are to conduct active recruiting programs designed to attract persons of outstanding qualifications.

6. The members of the boards are to be responsible for rating the applications which are received for examinations, and are likewise to be responsible for establishing eligible lists and certifying names from these lists for the filling of vacancies. These actions will all be subject to review by the commission.

7. Boards of examiners will hold examinations (a) for positions which are peculiar to a department or agency; (b) for positions which it is customary to fill by hiring at the gate; (c) for all positions in an establishment which is far removed from other federal agencies.

8. Where a position is peculiar to comparatively few agencies, a joint board of examiners will be established.

9. Where a position is common to all departments and agencies, the examination will be conducted through the Civil Service Commission's own offices.

There is nothing new about the philosophy underlying the establishments of these boards of examiners. Provision is made for such boards in the basic Civil Service Act passed in 1883. And for over sixty years skilled and semiskilled trades positions in government manufacturing establishments, such as government-operated navy yards and arsenals, have been filled in a very successful manner by examining boards located in these establishments.

We are providing now for the use of such boards in all occupational categories. And we are placing special emphasis on using these boards in the filling of professional, scientific, and technical positions.

This is not a paper program. Several hundred boards are

now in operation. During the fiscal year ending June 30, 1948, a large percentage of our total civil service appointments were made from lists of eligibles established by these boards of examiners.

In operating under this policy of decentralization, the Civil Service Commission is not divesting itself of responsibility for what happens in the field of recruitment. This we could not do under the law. This we could not do and preserve a genuine civil service system. We are saying, however, that we will discharge our responsibility by (a) setting standards; (b) delegating authority to act within those standards; and (c) checking up from time to time to make sure that there is adherence to standards.

And, on the whole, departments and agencies are apparently more than willing to follow a similar policy. During the war, in connection with their own operating responsibilities, departments and agencies delegated authority to act to bureaus, to sections, and to field establishments. At the same time, they made similar delegations of authority to act on personnel matters. Departments and agencies found that both types of delegation worked. In fact, most of them realized that if the delegations had not been made the machinery of government would have broken down. Consequently, in most instances the policy of decentralizing authority to act on personnel matters will be continued by the departments and agencies.

And so, in this manner, both the Civil Service Commission and the departments and agencies are making it possible for operating officials to participate directly in recruiting activities. Also, in this manner, we are speeding up the government's recruiting machinery compared with the manner in which it operated prior to the war.

All of this has definite implications as far as university education and the federal public service is concerned. It means, for example, that the responsibility for keeping in touch with the colleges and universities as a source of supply for the federal public service will be a joint responsibility resting upon the commission and the departments and agencies. It means that, in addition to personnel officials, a definite interest will be taken by operating officials in making appropriate contacts with colleges and universities. They will manifest this interest because they themselves will be playing a definite part in recruitment activities.

It also means that there will be increasing emphasis on contacts between the field offices of the commission and operating agencies, and the colleges and universities. That this is not idle speculation is shown by a very recent development out at the grass roots. The Civil Service Commission has a regional office at Denver, Colorado, which serves federal establishments in the states of Colorado, Utah, Wyoming, and New Mexico. The commission's regional director for that region has an advisory committee made up of administrators from government agencies, business organizations, and colleges and universities. Similar committees advise the commission's other regional directors. Out of this committee for the Denver region came a suggestion for the establishment of a college-federal service council.

Such a council has been organized. Operating heads of the principal federal agencies in the Denver region, and administrative officers of colleges and universities located within the region, are members of the council. The council has now provided for the establishment of committees on the social sciences, physical sciences, and biological sciences. These committees are made up of representatives of both federal agencies and colleges and universities.

This college-federal service council has established for itself the following objectives:

1. To acquaint college and university officials with the function of various federal agencies having opportunities for college-trained men and women in the federal service.

2. To study college curricula with the view to possible

changes to provide personnel better trained for federal employment.

3. To consider the addition of special courses for federal employees to broaden their training and to increase their effectiveness.

4. To develop the need for holding federal examinations so that senior students can attain eligibility and be selected for appointment to positions in the federal service before completing their college work, thus enabling the federal service to secure the services of top students.

There could not have been such a development prior to World War II. The reason is that neither the Civil Service Commission's regional office nor the regional offices of the departments and agencies would have had sufficient authority to act in the personnel field to make such a venture worthwhile. The commission has followed this project with great interest. It is convinced of its worthwhileness. As a result, similar developments are taking place in all of our regions. In addition, steps will undoubtedly be taken in the direction of setting up a similar group at the national level.

And here is another specific example. In the summer of 1946 the Board of U.S. Civil Service Examiners of the Air Materiel Command at Wright Field, Dayton, Ohio, announced a civil service examination for engineer, trainee. The announcement stated: "The duties of an engineer, trainee, will consist of a combination of (1) on-the-job training at Wright Field, and (2) scholastic training in engineering at a university designated by the Air Materiel Command. After successful completion of the program, trainees will be placed in engineering positions involving experimental research and development activities on aeronautical equipment and materiel."

As a result of this examination a very promising group of young men participated in a work-study program carried on in cooperation with the University of Cincinnati. In fact the project proved to be so successful that a similar examination was announced in the spring of 1947. Prior to the war there seemed to be insurmountable difficulties in the way of developing such a program. Decentralization has removed these obstacles.

Other specific examples could be given. It is clear, however, that decentralization of recruiting is sure to result in the development of much more effective working relationships between the university and the federal public service. And out of this close cooperation there should develop a better understanding of the federal public service on the part of college and university men and women.

One person after another who served in a key position during the war has come to us and said: "The public service needs a better public relations program. People do not understand it, and because they do not understand it, it is not held in the high esteem in which it should be held, if our government is to function effectively."

The point is well taken. The public service is not held in high esteem. And because it is not, we are constantly in danger of entrusting highly complex responsibilities to second-rate men. If we put second-rate men in the government's scientific laboratories, in important positions in the field of international relations, and in our key administrative posts, we are deliberately jeopardizing everything for which we fought in World War II. As never before in our history, top policy-making officials of the federal government must be supported by a career service made up of persons whose qualifications are second to none.

If our policy-making officials are to receive such support, the public service must be held in much higher esteem than it is today. To reach this goal we must, of course, keep improving the career service. And here are a few of the things that need to be done:

Civil Service Commission

1. We must pay higher salaries to our top professional, scientific, and administrative personnel. Our present ceiling of $10,000 on salaries for the career service should be lifted to at least $15,000.

2. We must provide opportunities for continued growth to those who are engaged in professional, scientific, and technical work. In-service training, leaves of absence for advanced study, as well as opportunities to observe how problems are handled outside of government, should all be included in such a program.

3. We must develop programs for promoting career servants which will minimize the possibility of such persons finding themselves in "dead-end" jobs. This is a difficult problem. In fact, it is so difficult that too often the public service has ignored it, instead of trying to work out a solution.

4. We must develop men and women who believe that the administrative job is a job of working with and developing human beings and not a job of reviewing papers.

But, even if all of these things are done, we will not achieve the objective we have in mind if the public generally does not know anything about the improvements that are made.

And that is the situation today. The career service has been improved. It is being improved. But very few persons know anything about the progress that has been made or that is being made. In fact, ignorance relative to the career service, both in and out of government, is appalling. For example, ask any ten persons you come in contact with if federal civil service employees can be and are fired for incompetence. All ten are almost sure to answer "No." And yet, during one year, 1946, more than 100,000 federal employees were discharged for cause. This figure does not include any of those who were laid off because of reduction in force.

There are many things that the federal government itself can do to offset this amazing lack of knowledge relative to the public service. And what the government can do, it should begin doing. It has no more important responsibility.

But, as colleges and universities come to have a closer working relationship with the public service, surely they also are going to do something to improve the situation. We have a right to expect that the university will take positive steps to provide those who are associated with it as students with at least an elementary knowledge of public service. Certainly a truly educated man should have such information about one of the most important of all our human institutions.

And, in this connection, let us not think alone of providing him with information about job opportunities in the public service, but let us place emphasis on providing him with information as to the manner in which the federal government, as an employer, actually functions. Then, even if the university student never enters the public service, he will go back to his home community and will be able to challenge the statements of the demagogue who can ply his trade so successfully by making wild attacks on the public service. In this way he can make a definite contribution to increasing the esteem in which the public service is held. Other students, as they learn about the public service, will see in it one of the finest opportunities that now exist for rendering constructive service to one's fellow human beings. They will respond to the challenge. And, as a result of their response, the levels of the public service will be constantly lifted.

Working hand in hand, and working out at the grass roots, the university and the public service can see to it that the public service is held in much higher esteem than it is today. It deserves, in spite of its imperfections, to be held in greater respect. And this is necessary if the democratic institutions in which we believe are to survive.

PART II

A TOP MANAGEMENT VIEW
OF THE FEDERAL SERVICE

4

THE TOP MANAGER AND HIS ENVIRONMENT

BY DONALD C. STONE

In this essay on the problems of top management, I have reference to the federal government primarily, although—making allowance for the effect of size—most of these observations apply also to state and local government. Indeed, they apply also to the rapidly mounting task of administering international organizations. I am using "top management" here to include both administrative and general staff positions. I am thinking of the heads of departments and agencies and their principal operating and staff assistants, and similar officials in the bureaus and other major subdivisions within departments. They are persons whose functions are almost entirely managerial or administrative, in contrast to "technical." Their energies are devoted broadly speaking to defining the objectives of their agencies, planning the program, developing an organization properly staffed to carry out the program, scheduling and budgeting the program, developing the necessary interrelationships, channels of communications, work habits, and doctrine for the organization to move forward as a harmonious team, establishing devices for control and coordination, exercising oversight and guiding the operations of the establishment, and maintaining and reacting to many external relationships.

Specifically, I propose to examine the setting in which the manager works, the forces with which he must contend, and the kind of person required for top management functions. In the main I shall leave to others the task of determining how the universities can best contribute to the development of individuals who possess the necessary knowledge, abilities, and personal characteristics for managerial leadership.

A major factor in the environment of the public manager is the relation of government to the people. We possess in this country, and fortunately so, certain basic concepts of the spiritual dignity, equality, and freedom of human beings. We view government as the servant of man, not its master. The public service is conditioned by the belief that the right to vote, hold office, and contribute to the conduct of government is a reflection of the social condition of equality, of freedom, and of opportunity. This has always been the promise of American life. Government institutions and government managers have always had to adjust to this underlying aspect of our culture.

Edwin L. Godkin in his work *Problems of Modern Democracy* refers to this element of our governmental environment in the following way: "The truth is that democracy is simply an experiment in the application of the principle of equality to the management of the common affairs of the community . . . rulers have become the mere hired servants of the mass of the community; and criticism of them has come naturally with the employment of them as agents."

The citizens of this country have decided through their elected representatives that they shall collectively carry on a vast range of activities to assure mutual protection, security, economic well being, convenience, and cultural development. The larger and more diverse the operations of government become, the more difficult it is to make them manageable and democratically responsive. Here we find a second major factor in the environment of the governmental manager.

The fact that there are approximately 2,000,000 full-time civilian employees on the federal payroll and that top managers are engaged in administering almost every type of activity or service imaginable gives only a partial clue to the character of the management job that must be done in order that all the resources of the nation may be most effectively mobilized for the purpose of carrying these programs forward.

The list of federal activities which the people, through their elected representatives, have determined must be carried out is almost endless. We find such diverse functions as military security and carrying the mail, the management of atomic energy and child labor regulations. We find the disposal of billions of dollars worth of surplus property and the education of Indians; extension of civil aviation and the granting of patents; the development of natural resources and the payment of veterans allowances; improvement of the public health and the conduct of foreign relations; assistance to farmers in increasing food production and the maintenance of lighthouses; the solution of industrial disputes and census taking; promotion of markets for American business and school lunch programs; ad infinitum.

The administration of these far-flung governmental functions, which falls upon the President and the top managers in the federal government, is a task perhaps unequaled in human experience. Certainly, it is unequaled in business. A high officer of the government recently remarked that he encountered every day as many major policy or administrative problems as he had observed in large businesses over a period of a year. Indeed, what may give us most faith in the character of our political institutions and in the fundamental philosophy of life which supports them is the fact that under the most adverse circumstances these diverse operations are successfully administered. Military victory was not secured because we had vast resources, although the resources were essential. It was achieved because we were able, under our political structure, to mobilize the necessary administrative resources for the tasks we had to do. The study of captured documents on German, Italian, and Japanese war administration dispels quickly the once-prevalent notion that efficiency can be achieved more readily in a dictatorship than in a democracy.

Donald C. Stone

When we were matched against the "impossible" task of catching up with the enemy's long head start, it was found that we not only possess a reservoir of managerial talent superior to that of any of the dictatorships but also that we have other ingredients in our tradition which enable government to function under the most unfavorable conditions, and this despite our supposed inability to mobilize for war as continuously reported by enemy intelligence.

Top management in government works in an environment of instability. Identification of a few of the factors which contribute to this situation may serve to give us a clue to the kind of persons required for this work. In a democracy the citizen is the boss. Through his freedom to say what he thinks, to organize politically, to throw out the incumbent and put a new man in, and to join with others who have related interests to press for a particular purpose, he can bring great pressure not only on policies and political leadership but upon top managers and on officials all the way down the line. His influence affects vitally day-to-day administrative action—not just at election time.

The fact that the public official is an employee of the citizen in a real and not just a sentimental sense provides the citizen with a fertile field for public review and criticism. Too often this takes the form of personal abuse, and even public insult bordering on the scandalous. The impulse to "shoot the pianist" may have nothing to do with his performance but rather with a dislike of the tune selected for him. Human nature expressing itself as it does, there is a tendency among bosses to look down on their employees; the public is no exception. Some of this criticism is healthy. Much of it is destructive and serves to intimidate all but the bold in the fearless performance of their responsibilities. Sniping from behind the back by persons whose motives may or may not be sincere is disturbing; no conscientious and honest government executive is afraid of responsible criticism.

The political nature of government with cleavages encouraged by the separation of powers in our federal system further contributes to the instability of the top management environment. Management must adjust its sights continuously as political objectives change. It must function in a manner acceptable to the majority of those who come in contact with the agency's operations, and in addition, it must often placate individuals who desire to discredit its program.

The manner in which the committee system of Congress works and the absence of real party responsibility and discipline can easily result in a small group or even a single committee member being able to force an agency to pursue policies which would not be sustained by the Congress as a whole. This is natural because a member of Congress is an important person. His constituents look to him for action when they don't like the way things are done. He should individually, as well as collectively, exercise great *influence* in getting things done right as he sees them. It is when he tries to *decide* governmental action on an individual basis that sound legislative-executive relations are disturbed. Agency management will often find itself attacked by the party opposed to the administration, and yet the party in power whose program is being carried out may not rise to the agency's defense. Criticism of the executive branch frequently congeals more quickly within Congress than does the support of members of the President's party for the agencies responsible for carrying out administration policies.

All of this weakens the actual authority reposing in the President and agency top management and undermines their positions. There are always problems wholly within management's formal scope of authority which it will assiduously avoid at certain times, or at all times. Shifting legislative alignments, a law people will not accept, the rise and fall of popular movements, personal misunderstandings between management offi-

Donald C. Stone

cials and other public figures, impending elections, and an adverse press are part of the "facts of life" to top management. Any one of these might tip the scales to prevent management from doing what it ought to do. Management must, therefore, keep its radar instruments screening the horizon for signs of shifts in public opinion, of conflicts and personal ambitions of politicians, and of the status of special interests, lest it be engulfed by open attacks from without or sabotage from within. This does not mean that management must operate politically or be politically motivated, although it must at all times be subordinate to politicians. On the other hand, top managers need to be politically sophisticated and sensitive, keeping their guard rails set against pressure for improper action and entanglements on the one hand, and maintaining a position of integrity and impartiality, on the other.

The governmental managerial official is called upon to devote a far larger proportion of his time to justifying his program and operations than his counterpart outside the government. Many officials complain that they must spend so much time in preparing for appearing at Congressional hearings and in presenting their programs before the Bureau of the Budget and other bodies that it often leaves little time for directing the operations of their agencies. Also, the necessity for checking proposed actions and for keeping complete records of their activities in case they must defend themselves absorbs a great deal of time which otherwise might be devoted to more constructive effort. All in all, it is small wonder that most government officials are found at their desks long after closing time or carry home a brief case of papers which "one of those days" prevented them from reviewing. Arthur Krock, in the *New York Times Magazine* of December 9, 1945, gives a vivid picture of the demands upon the time of agency heads in an article "Washington Hasn't Enough Time to Think."

The governmental manager has frequently been described as operating in a goldfish bowl. His every act is not only subject to inspection, publicity, and criticism, but in the absence of "Marquis of Queensbury rules," his personal as well as his official life may be attacked with the aim of creating suspicion or discrediting him publicly. And he must grin and bear it. He may be made the scapegoat even though he makes an honest and responsible attempt to carry out public policy. Some dissident element in the population may vilify him because his agency's program runs counter to personal greed. Half-truths and unfair insinuations may appear in the press or on the radio. Some of the criticism grows out of antipathy for any kind of responsible government or at least antipathy for the idea of the government rendering service to the "whole" people.

For this privilege of being pushed about, we pay top management a paltry sum. The federal civil service ceiling is $10,000. This sum is paid to officials responsible for operations many times larger and more complex than are found in the biggest private corporation. There may be two, three, four, or even five levels of responsible positions under the head of any agency or large subdivision that are also paid at this rate. This is necessary because there are so few salary or grade levels. It is small wonder that key officials become unwilling, with increasing frequency, to let their devotion to the public service offset the small financial reward and the heavy responsibility their posts entail. The fact that the great majority stick at their job faithfully is mute testimony of the extent to which public work appeals to the hearts and minds of many persons.

Even more frustrating perhaps to top management are the resistances—passive and overt—within the organization. Unreconciled differences and points of view among the staff may nullify managerial leadership. Specialists asserting particular interests may block the achievement of broader objectives. The deadening effort of routine and tradition may have so ossified the organization that jogging it off dead center may fall in the category of a miracle. Incompetence or disloyalty in key units of the organization may seriously detract from their value to top management. Perhaps most serious of all hindrances is the tendency of human nature to express itself in ways which prevent individuals from working easily with others toward organizational objectives. These resistances to progress are in part the inevitable result of trying to mobilize a large number of human beings to a common end. Governmental employees are like other human beings and present a wide range of mental and emotional traits. Few persons in an organization, public or private, are ideal for the particular positions they hold. Relatively greater shortcomings inevitably exist in government than in most other enterprises because of the infinitely greater difficulty and demands of its work. I have heard a federal official, in despairing over his personnel difficulties, make the remark that a governmental department is the only kind of mental institution managed by its inmates.

The essential element to bear in mind is that an organization consists of men working in relationship to each other. No matter how scientifically the structural arrangements may be worked out and its objectives and programs defined, no matter how carefully the persons are selected to fill the various positions, its existence as an organization in a working sense is not necessarily achieved. It is achieved, as Chester Barnard has often pointed out, *only* when almost all the efforts of the persons comprising the organization are the result of experience of working in concert, have become a matter of habit and tradition, and are conditioned to the environmental factors surrounding them. Each employee must assimilate as part of his reaction patterns the methods, behavior, and responses of all other employees with whom he has contact. There can be no intelligent communication and understanding among the members of an organization until they have worked together on a trial and error basis under the stimulus of a management alert to the necessity of harmonizing human relationships. The organization must become literate and articulate; otherwise, the behavior dialect of employees will be incomprehensible one to the other. The spontaneous relationships that derive from human cooperation are essential elements in organization. They determine whether it will function well, or at all. The insecurity that pervades the fast changing governmental scene makes harmonious working relationships especially hard to achieve. Although working relationships may be easily disrupted for the same reason, the momentum which an organization gathers when all parts have learned to pull together testifies to the significant part which habitual behavior plays in administration. Some agencies which have been well organized continue to carry out their functions effectively for long periods after losing progressive leadership and active popular support for their program.

Let us look at some of the other forces that play upon top management from within the public service. Authority is not self-enforcing. It never equals in scope the legal mandate given the head of an agency, and its scope varies according to the condition of the organization and the state of mind of the employees, as well as outside circumstances. All too often we view management as achieving its ends through the exercise of directive power. Buttons are pressed; orders go down the line; men spring into action. Nothing is more remote from the truth. Instead of being in a position to dictate, top management is more generally the prisoner of the organization.

Management cannot secure its aims on a command basis. While there are occasions when management must decide against the preponderate view of the staff, it can make such decisions only rarely. Otherwise it will lose the confidence of the organization. The employees must understand what is expected of them and know how to carry out the policies, administrative arrangements, and other requirements or they will necessarily work ineffectively and at cross purposes. Man carries along a heavy load of conformity, but he does not

necessarily function as a cog in a complex team. His individ-
ualistic urges militate against organization. However, under
proper stimulus most persons find satisfaction in teamwork.
This cannot be derived, however, from a police basis of supervision. Teamwork entails the wholehearted participation of
the members of the team. Most employees will respond if they
see the validity of a course of action and are convinced of the
integrity of those who lead. The job of management is therefore to exercise such leadership as will produce spontaneous
and cooperative effort rather than to try to impose arbitrary
decisions. The cooperation of individuals within an organization can only be won by ever renewed effort.

Invariably the channels through which management functions and the interrelationship of the several units in governmental establishments differ from what one might deduce from
the regular and hierarchical arrangement of boxes on an organization chart. Among the factors which cause this are the
inadequacy of some of the individuals to carry their full load
of participation and the exceptional trustworthiness of others,
the inherently greater importance of some offices although they
may be equally subordinate to a single superior, the extent
to which a unit has many or few relationships with other units
in the organization, the degree of public interest in a unit, and
the potential trouble which the operations of a unit might give
if not kept under special surveillance. The necessity of working around a dissident staff until they can be reconciled, re-
formed, or removed contributes to informal arrangements
which may be disrupting, unless understood by the other participants.

The problem of organizing a governmental office is in large
measure a continuous process of getting everyone to understand
how they fit into it, what is expected of them, who they must
consult or advise, and the limitations of their discretion. However, tradition often places a dead hand upon governmental
organizations. Habitual practice, established procedures,

standard routines are essential but unless employees all the way down the line as well as top management are alert to change, always looking for a better way, ossification sets in. This may lead to the defeat of any new idea and the mangling of the intent of administrative instruction. It is no minor feat to shove an old governmental institution off established precedent, or to discover the secret of compensating for weaknesses in one set of channels by using other perhaps less orthodox channels without disrupting the works.

Top management can convey many a good idea to the staff if it goes about it in the right manner, but it cannot issue an order and have it successfully applied down the line if the staff doesn't believe in it. It is no secret that administrative orders may completely change their meaning while traveling from one level of authority to another (if they travel at all). In the average situation in government, top management cannot fire very many persons, not because there may be political repercussions but because the organization can't "take it." Management can overrule subordinates once in a while on recommendations and reports, but as a usual thing they cannot tamper in a major way with documents which come to them for signature. General Pershing's reported comment in a moment of frustration during World War I, "How many colonels have I got to make to get this done?" illustrates the point. In the light of these varied obstacles to quick and effective execution of governmental programs, we can see that the life of those in top management positions is hardly a bed of roses.

However, I do not want to draw a purely negative picture. The manager can do many things to keep on top of his organization. I shall not elaborate, but there may be mentioned in passing the power of appointment and removal, the power of review and determination, establishment of a plan of organization which throws major issues up to the top, general staff assistance, and systematic internal and external "intelligence"—not to mention the influence which a stouthearted, persuasive, and sincere man skilled in human relations may have upon his organization.

Unfortunately many participants in the top management of federal departments and agencies do not possess the necessary abilities to exercise these authorities well and the extraordinary personal traits needed to cope with their environment. If I were to generalize about the persons comprising the top management group in the federal government, however, I would say that they are on the whole a conscientious group thoroughly devoted to the public interest. While they constitute in most respects a cross section of American citizens and are subject to the same strengths and weaknesses of character and ability, I believe on the whole they reflect a higher level of idealism and devotion to purposes beyond their personal ambitions and acquisitiveness than is found in private business. While they may flinch when branded as "parasites," "communists," "payrollers," or when charged with having the sole aim of advancing their personal positions and whims, they usually shrug their shoulders, dig in at the job with increased energy, and produce on the whole a creditable performance. The number who are politically ambitious or who attempt to advance the special interests of one party or group at the expense of another is surprisingly small.

My principal criticism would be that too few of them were recruited as a result of a positive and persevering program to procure the best talent that exists in the country, and that too many of them possess insufficient variety and breadth of experience within and without the government to enable them to cope to best advantage with the complexities of their jobs. Greater understanding of political, social, and cultural forces which are at play within this country and within the world is necessary, and greater knowledge and skill in the art and science of management are parallel essentials.

Let us examine more intensively this question of what kinds

of persons are required for top management work. I say kinds because obviously many types of qualifications and skills are needed. There can be no stereotype. A man who succeeds in an operating job may fail at staff work; and the same is true for fast-moving *vs.* slow-moving programs; public-contact *vs.* internal-contact jobs; principal *vs.* deputy roles; and many other varieties of managerial conditions.

"Breadth" is obviously one of the first characteristics required of persons who deal with the complex and managerial situations I have described. The broad purposes which government must achieve involve the utilization of many disciplines, professional skills, and fields of knowledge. Governmental processes and action have almost limitless ramifications and repercussions in their impact upon the culture, economy, social aspirations, political behavior, and morale of citizens—individually and corporately.

Rowland Egger, a keen observer of contemporary problems, relates, in the booklet, *University Bureaus of Public Administration,* published by the University of Alabama, how the question of opening a highway through the University of Virginia campus was a sociological and geo-political problem of the first magnitude. The potential effect of the proposal upon the pattern of economic, social, and political power in the community had, with much recrimination, delayed the street opening for a long time. Final action on the project, according to Egger, contributed directly or indirectly to two divorces, one bankruptcy, five lawsuits, an effort to abolish the city manager plan, and the establishment of a new church. It revived a down-at-heel family to the point that two homely daughters captured husbands. It led to the election of a college professor to the city council, which, in turn, resulted in a slum clearance movement that broke the grip of a local political boss whose business was the rental of slum properties to Negroes. It changed, in a relatively short time, the political control of the municipality. Subsequently, a complicated set of negotiations

Donald C. Stone

of federal-state-local character were required since the street was a link in state highway and federal-aid road programs. In addition, a variety of engineering, construction, maintenance, legal, and financial problems was encountered involving federal, state, municipal, and university relationships.

The question arises whether, in the light of this illustration, we leave the responsibility for handling the administrative affairs of government to engineers, physicians, physicists, social workers, militarists, or transportation experts, whose orientation and training are technical and specialized, or whether we place such responsibility in the hands of persons who have their roots deep into the whole range of human knowledge and human relationships. In this context we see more clearly how public administrators are about the only persons whose responsibilities require them to utilize all fields of knowledge and all types of skills in carrying on their work. This breadth of understanding and interest by top management is required not only in the over-all direction of a government or of a broad department, but it is also essential at the bureau and divisional levels.

Unless the head of a foreign trade office, for example, has a wide understanding of social, economic, and political problems both at home and abroad, he cannot deal effectively with the major questions of foreign trade. An understanding of the problem of trade in any commodity requires an appreciation of production and distribution, security, engineering, financial, geological, transportation, and many other factors. No matter how broad his knowledge and experience or how skillful in dealing with people, the competent generalist must, of course, master a sufficient amount of the technical subject matter over which he may have responsibility so that he can harness the specialists and maintain control over his organization. This is not as difficult as it sounds. Many generalists with administrative ability have demonstrated that they can move from top management positions in one functional field to another with confidence and success. Indeed, demonstration of ability to do this is the only adequate proof of ability to take on any new job. Success in one might be attributable to many supporting factors.

On the other hand, to the extent that the specialist is having to deal with other than the purely technical considerations of his specialty—and this includes most employees of government in the higher brackets—he must come to understand something about the social-political-economic environment within which his particular responsibilities are carried out if he is to be more than a lone worker in a cell. The tendency of the specialist to apply the criteria of his special subject to other subjects than his specialty often produces dogmatism, prejudice, and narrow-mindedness, particularly toward other large fields. He tends to oversimplify the problems of government. This not only limits seriously his usefulness in an administrative organization but also his contribution as a citizen in community affairs. The cumulative effect of this common tendency among specialists can easily crush the spirit of an entire organization if resourceful leadership is not provided by top management.

Viewed in this light, public administration embraces infinitely more than the policies, processes, and techniques of administration, broad as this subject matter is. It requires competence in synthesizing and applying many disciplines in carrying out public purposes, and in the mobilization and use of a vast array of skills and techniques to achieve these purposes. It calls for sensitiveness to public reactions, responsiveness, considerateness, a sense of the feasible.

John Dewey, in *The Public and Its Problems,* detected twenty years ago what the role of public administration should be. He came to the conclusion that it is not a self-contained entity, but a tool through the use of which society can solve certain of its problems. It is not an end in itself but a means for achieving social purposes, and hence those who practice this

Donald C. Stone

calling must have full grasp of all matters which condition its use.

How different has been the approach to public administration in the universities. For the most part, it has been viewed as a specialized aspect of other specialized fields. Frequently a few courses have been added to the political science curriculum on the assumption that public administration is a segment of political science.

Similarly, many universities have proceeded on the basis that, if a person is trained in specialized management subjects, such as administrative law, budgeting, purchasing, personnel, reporting, governmental structure, and coordination and control mechanisms, he is trained in the art and science of public management. (Most curricula in public administration ignore the operating side of government, particularly in its major functional fields.) I am not questioning the value of such training, particularly when broadly conceived. I simply wish to emphasize that it is only a small part of the essential equipment.

To overcome this insular approach, the universities must first of all recognize the nature of the society in which we live today and the role and methods of public administration in society, including the resources of the social scientist for analysis and interpretation.

In the light of such understanding, would it not be fruitful for the universities to concentrate on training two broad classes of citizens? First, persons who can be expected with experience to tackle the more difficult phases of the world's work either as political or top management leaders; second, specialists in the particular segments of the world's work who also possess sufficient orientation in the nature, processes, and goals of our society to enable them to become effective generalists, at least in this more restricted field. Does this not also call for a recognition that only a small proportion of university graduates will be required for purposes of scientific investigation and research? Most of them will be called upon to engage in the various professions and trades, within and without government.

If we move forward in this direction, we may need not only a drastic reorganization of our thinking but also of the organization and curricula of our universities. I am not implying that all research and teaching should be directed toward public administration and the development of persons who are equipped to play responsible roles in current day society. Far be it from that. But is it not the great challenge of the university to provide a suitable background and understanding on the part of students who aim to become either specialists or generalists which will enable them to take an increasingly responsible part in contemporary life? Are we not at a minimum confronted here with the problem of how to harness all branches of the university in a manner which will enable each to contribute in training potential managerial and political leaders as well as in prosecuting the more specialized ends for which each branch was established?

But a great deal more than knowledge secured within or without the university is required to carry out the mission of top management in government. A manager must be a person who can negotiate with people, who can deal skillfully with and through people, get decisions nailed down. He must mold an institution which taps the contributions of specialists, utilizes all fields of knowledge, and produces a satisfactory and acceptable end product.

The top manager must combine strength of mind with skill in diplomacy. He must intuitively judge political forces, situations, and personalities in order to make the most of the temperamental winds of politics and group reactions. He may never escape compromise of issues but he must be capable of doing so without compromising himself. Above all, in a democracy, he must have a sure sense of the public interest and the ability to discern clearly the line leading from the prag-matic considerations of the immediate present to the long-range objective which has been staked out to meet the needs of the citizenry at large.

Intelligence and knowledge will not alone provide skill and competence in such matters as these. The managers must be persons of character—individuals who possess a body of ideals and purposes adequate to cope with powerful current day forces toward social disintegration and friction. They must embody sufficient moral integrity to win the confidence of those with whom they come in contact both within their organiza-tions and without. A person who is unadjusted in his personal relationships, who is self-centered, arrogant, greedy, intolerant, intellectually dishonest, or unfaithful will not exercise con-structive leadership and effective influence over his organiza-tion for long no matter how clever he is. If others are to respond positively, the scale of values which govern his life must reflect the moral requisites that God has established as the basis for our human brotherhood. If a top manager tries to run against the grain of life, it crosses him up and he crosses up all of his relationships. This may not always be evident at first but the disease spreads like a cancer until the individual loses his grip and becomes a defeated person.

An official said to me the other day that the greatest weak-ness in top management was an unwillingness to deal honestly with issues which require courage to resolve. Perhaps this is not surprising because the proportion of persons who deal frankly and truthfully in all aspects of their relations with others seems very small.

It is my belief that the main difficulty in top management in government is one of character. Indeed, is this not the key problem the world round? Too many men try to live entirely off their own resources and govern their actions by what is expedient or what will advance their material or personal desires. They set themselves up as gods. Without resources beyond themselves which give meaning and coherence to life and which sustain them in meeting their daily problems, they become defeated and sour, full of inner conflicts, uncertainties, and fears. The greater the responsibility, the greater is the need of top managers for a philosophy of life which will sustain them no matter what the trials and difficulties of their environment. If they possess this, they will not be frustrated individuals. If they are truly frustrated, they cannot be good managers.

Here again we see the role of the university in an old light but also one that is often forgotten. Must not the university, in its relation to the public service, be concerned with more than teaching, and the students devoted to securing more than knowledge and skill? If this were not so we might conclude that the goal of education is to train students to outstrip their associates professionally, to get ahead in position, to gain wealth, in short to be a success as the world views success.

Must we not, in short, view the aims of the university from the standpoint of what it can contribute to sustaining and supporting a society in which democracy and freedom can flourish and in which man can attain his highest fulfillment? Does this not mean that an overriding goal must be to develop in oncoming generations the highest qualities of character? Would not any lesser primary goal lead to an undermining of our civilization as well as to individual frustration and bitterness because tomorrow's leaders would lack not only a synthesis of knowledge but a synthesis of life without which there can be no realization of their higher potentialities?

5

A BUSINESS EXECUTIVE
LOOKS AT GOVERNMENT

BY ROBERT A. LOVETT

IN ANY consideration of government operations, whether by businessmen or educators, I think certain characteristics of the federal government must be kept constantly in mind. Most of these are so obvious as to be tiresome. But they constituted rediscovered truisms to many experienced managers who entered government service during the war. And failure to recognize them was a frequent cause of the unhappy experiences and the bumper crop of gastric ulcers of men who had records of high competence in private business.

Government as it now exists is a vast enterprise involving several million employees at various levels of responsibility. It is the nation's largest employer of labor. It deals with practically every phase of the daily life of the public. It is, in fact, a large group of people dealing with larger human problems. Therefore, it is extremely complex. As a consequence of its large size and multiple activities, it is wholly unrealistic to talk of making government simple. We can aspire to make it manageable and effective but I think it has to be rather complex just as in a lesser way the manufacture of automobiles is complex. Oversimplification has been labeled by the former Director of the Budget, Harold Smith, as the "number one stumbling block to the solution of any problem." Another characteristic of federal service is the existence of an inevitable difference of interests between departments and frequently between bureaus within a department. Such divergence of interest is normal, and arises out of the necessity to reconcile the different needs of various groups of citizens. One of the primary tasks of management is, therefore, to provide the machinery and the conditions under which conflicting interests present recognizable issues which can be promptly decided.

Most important among these examples of special conditions surrounding government is the basic distinguishing characteristic of the public servant—the fact that the government executive is the guardian of the public interest and that in accepting this responsibility he accepts accountability to the public, directly or indirectly, for his actions. As a consequence, he must be prepared for a continuous, detailed, and suspicious supervision by Congress, the press, and the public. This condition was reluctantly accepted by many businessmen in government; and it has become a more familiar, if sometimes irritating, concept to many businessmen outside of government.

The combination of the foregoing factors—size, complexity, conflicts of interest, and constant accountability to the public— has resulted in great emphasis on organization, method, and routines to meet the need for dealing with public pressures, for adapting action to the decisions of legislative bodies, and for establishing operating procedures within the rigid limits imposed by laws and executive regulations.

Indeed, no matter how well briefed on federal service peculiarities the private business executive may be, one of the first things he notices in public administration is this emphasis on procedure and routine. This emphasis is admittedly necessary and desirable provided it does not make method an end in itself. When it does, overorganized bewilderment results.

The newcomer to top management positions in the federal service frequently feels that the organization and methods set up with the laudable idea of keeping him from doing wrong actually result in making it excessively difficult to do right. Furthermore, it is this same preoccupation with procedure and paper work that has, I suspect, caused a second phenomenon in federal service—the surprisingly large number of specialists, technicians, and experts in government. This turned out to be rather fortunate in the crisis caused by war except insofar as overemphasis on the specialist contributed to underemphasis on the generalist and trained manager. The latter were in relatively scarce supply. I say "relatively scarce" because there were, scattered throughout government agencies, a number of extremely competent public administrators. But they were far harder to find than specialists. It was this imbalance that caused a harassed and sardonic secretary who was searching for a general staff assistant to say that, if all the specialists and technicians in Washington were placed end to end, they ought to be left that way.

Essentially the crucial problem of government administration is the same as that of private business—the getting of good men and fitting the proper man into the job. Efforts to get first class personnel into the executive agencies became the number one problem of management. Its solution called for a liberal interpretation of civil service rules and requirements by the Civil Service Commission and the development of certain new and decentralized procedures in connection with the recruitment of personnel. The fact that a moderately decentralized system was developed during the war was not only proof of the cooperative efforts of the commissioners but also an indication that an improved system embodying certain desirable aspects of wartime practice may be possible in peacetime. While civil service showed some adaptability in meeting the enormous requirements for personnel in the lower grades, the system was not equipped, in my opinion, to meet the needs for the higher grades. I doubt if ten per cent of top grades in wartime came through civil service machinery. Had it not been for the direct efforts of sincere officials to persuade their outside associates to lend a hand in federal service the tremendous job of staffing the agencies could not have been done.

In civil service regulations, I think we find the same factor noted above in connection with organization and method. Here again we find that the need for protection against wrongdoing has received more attention than has the provision of means for doing right. Admittedly, the problem of balance is exceedingly difficult but I believe it can be cured, and I am informed that certain constructive steps are already under way. But I question whether our civil service system is aimed at the right target. Some students of the problem have suggested that our system is designed to protect the electorate from bribery by appointments from a political party, whereas in England the pressure was to protect civil servants from political corruption. I am not qualified to express an opinion on the merits of such observations, but I think there is fairly general agreement among the wartime administrators obtained from private business that our civil service system constituted a major problem in their efforts to set up an effective organization in a period of crisis.

On the credit side of the federal service and its personnel policies we must note the great improvement in compensation levels in the lower and middle groups of federal workers. In the recent past, salaries in groups below, say, $7,000 per annum have raised to a level that compares very favorably with private business. In certain categories rates are higher. As a result, the routine machinery provided by government, judging by experience in the War Department, compared favorably with a good private office in peacetime. But the top professional scientific and administrative groups have not been similarly treated as to salary adjustment. The natural result of this is that the experience and training of the most competent persons are frequently lost to private employers at about the time when the greatest return to the government should be forthcoming. I do not mean to imply that government can or should compete with private business in administrative officers' salaries. In my opinion, it should not. On the other hand, it should be more realistic in meeting changed economic conditions and not let virtue wear itself out in being its own reward.

Robert A. Lovett

This salary question focuses attention on one of the real difficulties faced by top management and the government—the lack of adequate continuity in the administrative levels of most executive agencies. The normal turnover under our form of government as a result of changes in party administration presents a moderate amount of difficulty in maintaining efficiency and in the execution of long-range plans. It is aggravated by the low compensation in the top administrative categories. Perhaps this situation can be improved by including in the responsible manager's office a relatively permanent top staff assistant. The War Department established the position of Administrative Assistant to the Secretary of War in 1931. This position has been continued under four different secretaries during the past fifteen years.

In an effort to obtain the advantage of continuity, I think the government must guard against the temptations of the closed career service, either in the government as a whole or in any part such as the foreign service or the military. There should most certainly be a career service. It is the closed aspect that seems to me to be objectionable. I think it should be flexible enough as regards required training and opportunity for entrance above the beginning grade so that competition at all levels will encourage vitality and growth. Government today is far too complex to enable any group to know all the answers. Here again, business experience also would militate against a "closed career service" if a fresh approach and initiative are to be preserved.

Last among this partial list of problems comes that terrible matter of coordination. I had hoped to avoid the word because "coordinator" became an epithet rather than a title. Men who were otherwise patient and reasonable and who would readily admit the need for coordination in a machine so huge, so complex, and so divergent in interests and objectives, would roar with frustration when subjected to it. In fact, one of these bitter and now familiar definitions which helped blow off steam ran something like this: a coordinator is a man who brings organized chaos out of regimented confusion.

Coordination within one's own department was easily appreciated and was, in most cases, not hard to obtain. But coordination between several government departments was fantastically difficult even under the pressure of war. The Committee of Three, the State War and Navy Coordinating Committee, and the Air Coordinating Committee, with their special secretariats, were examples of attempts to meet the problem and they helped a great deal. But they were improvisations to meet an urgent need. It is still too easy for one government department to stall action in another, or several others, by neither agreeing nor disagreeing. This is the often-criticized technique known as "dragging the feet." I suggest that this problem stems from a lack of effective machinery for top policy control—a result of the vast increase in government functions that in turn has made coordination in the cabinet physically impossible. This problem again is present in large-scale businesses but, because government is so much bigger and more complex, the need for coordination in the latter is much greater.

So much for some of the problems faced by management. Since it has been necessary to mention them, I think it is only fair at this point to say that, in my opinion, government did an excellent job of administration during the war. Our system of government stood the critical test of world-wide conflict and ably performed its dual obligation—to get results and to get them with the least disturbance to the ideal of democracy. Government showed ability to correct mistakes as it went along and constantly to improve its effectiveness without losing sight of its main objective—victory as quickly as possible. Perhaps I attach special significance to this self-corrective characteristic of a flexible democracy. If so, it is because of the deep impression made on me in May and June of 1945 when,

Robert A. Lovett

during an inspection of the remnants of the German Wehrmacht, I had ample proof that the vaunted efficiency of a dictatorship of the German type was an exploded myth. The carefully documented testimony of Dr. Albert Speer showed that German governmental management was very inefficient in many vital respects and that the reason was identifiable. This reason was the unwillingness to admit mistakes in planning, production, and use of material through fear; the covering up of errors by the petty dictators placed over various projects and industries; and because of these factors, the perpetuation of errors. Ruthlessness did not prove to be a substitute for responsibility to the public.

And now let us consider briefly some of the desirable attitudes and the deficiencies of top management that could be observed in government administration during the war. Attention has been repeatedly called to the shortage of broad-gauge managers by numerous government officials, notably from the Bureau of the Budget, under whose guidance so much has been done to improve quality and training of personnel and federal administration in general. The need for good men was partly satisfied by drawing on private business, but the effectiveness of these men as federal executives was often delayed and made more difficult by a common deficiency. Too many did not have an adequate appreciation of the special characteristics and problems of public administration and too few had any real working knowledge of governmental organization as a whole and the relationship of his department to others. This may have been the result of personal indifference or a lack in our system of education, or both. Whatever the reason, it made more work for everybody. The newly sworn-in administrator added much vitality to administration and he generally learned fast; but when he approached the job with the attitude that "everything in government is terrible" and tried to run his office as he did when he was head of the National Bustle and Flute Corporation, he became a first-class headache. Fortunately, this was the exception. Yet it points up, I think, two of the major needs today: (1) a wider understanding of the problems of government by businessmen; and (2) the desirability of working out some sort of triple interchange of personnel between business and government, between the universities and government, and between business and the universities.

The selection of a staff is, of course, one of the most important series of decisions that top management must make. Since the object of this staff is to extend the planning, coordinating, and control capabilities of top management, the choice of personnel must be related to the manager's special requirements. A deficiency in the manager can be largely cured by an able staff assistant to fill that gap. Some managers, it must be added, were reluctant to admit any shortcomings. In the selection of a staff there were two functions that were frequently overlooked. They deserve, I believe, more attention than is generally accorded them. The first of these is the maintenance of liaison, externally with other agencies and internally with bureaus or divisions of the manager's own department. As a corollary there is the task of advising the executive on relationships with the public. The second advisory function is that of checking everything for the *facts*. There is so much rumor and so much passionate advocacy, that the only safeguard is a strict top-level insistence on all the facts, favorable and unfavorable, before reaching a decision. This search for and insistence on facts is a full-time job for an able and courageous assistant.

The other staff assistants can be selected in considerable part from among numerous specialists in government and in business, after the manager has familiarized himself with the facilities of management available to him. Certain agencies, such as the War Department, were well supplied with advisory staff personnel to supplement the civilian secretariat and the operating personnel. Thanks to the foresight of Elihu Root, New-

ton Baker, and Henry Stimson, the army had officers specially
trained for administration in graduates of the Command and
General Staff School, the War College and the Industrial College. The technical branches have had for years, in addition to
this in-service training, the advantage of postgraduate work in
universities in subjects ranging from those covered by the leading scientific schools to those of the graduate business schools
and schools of political science. In those agencies that have not
been so fortunate in having their own supply of trained men,
it has generally been easier to find people in the government
service who know how to assist with some aspect of administration or coordination than to find people trained in administration itself. This situation has caused the frequent suggestion
that more of the civilian agencies similarly be given a chance
to sponsor postgraduate work in civil service and that the government concentrate more effort in developing and providing
in-service training for higher administration.

We have so far considered a few of the difficulties faced by
the federal administrator and executive during wartime, as
well as a few of the special long-range problems observed when
outside managers were introduced into government management. In summary, the list we noted covered the following observations: (1) great emphasis on procedure and paper work;
(2) the shortage of trained line and operating administrators
at top and intermediate supervisory levels as compared with the
availability of specialists; (3) the great and growing need for
good men throughout government; (4) the difficulties in filling
the higher grades under our civil service system and its basic
rigidity; (5) the problem of adequate pay in the higher grades
(although pay in the lower and middle groups compares favor-
ably with nongovernment work); (6) the difficulty of maintaining continuity in the top administrative levels; (7) the problem
of the closed career service; (8) the overriding difficulty of coordination under our present improvised system; (9) the need
for maintaining liaison between executive agencies; (10) the

lack of adequate understanding by administrators from outside government of the special characteristics of the government problem; (11) ignorance of government organization; (12) importance of staff assistants; and finally, the need for special training both by in-service and by postgraduate work.

Some of these concern the structure of government; others particularly concern personnel. In the light of these observations it becomes apparent that able men with a common purpose and good will toward each other can make even a cumbersome system work. Naturally it could work much better if it were freed from some of the obstacles to full effectiveness. But any system will need the best possible public servant to run it.

So we come now to what I think is a fundamental question: Why don't more of this country's ablest men go into government service? In an effort to get a composite suggestion, I have communicated with six men who served as federal administrators during the war in various departments and have since returned to private life. Several questions were asked as to their own experience and the majority of their points are covered in the items already discussed. There was a high degree of unanimity on blasts at red-tape, antiquated methods of coordination, lack of top policy control, and so forth. This was expected with allowances for differences in emphasis. What was not expected was the surprising similarity in the answers to the following question: "What do you think are the main deterrents to able young men entering federal service or continuing in it?"

All the answers touched on pay and the lack of security in the higher administrative jobs caused by the changes normally following a shift in national administration. The majority of answers stressed the point that many men felt that government service was not a respected profession. The reasons have often been advanced. A somewhat novel viewpoint was expressed in several replies which pointed out that especially among older men and those already established in professions, a deterring factor was fear on the part of the individual that, no matter how blameless he is, he may be used as a target to get headlines by some sensation-seeking politician. Typical of this point of view is the following excerpt from one of the replies: "I believe that a great many good men are deterred from going into responsible positions in the Federal service because of fear that, through no fault of their own, they may some day be pilloried by politicians on investigating committees or elsewhere. I do not mean by this that congressional investigating committees should be abolished. They are an essential part of our American governmental machinery and they do much to keep the wayward on the straight and narrow path. Their power is enormous and it must be so. On the other hand, the very fact that their power is so great should make them use it as trustees, with meticulous care never to prejudice the interests or career of the honest, sincere man." He went on to say that, in extreme cases, loose and unjust charges cause the individual involved to do nothing in order to avoid being accused of doing something. Whether the views of these men are colored by the circumstances of their service in wartime or whether they are more widely held, I am, of course, unable to say. It is, however, frank and interesting testimony and it invites attention to a situation which I think lies at the bottom of many of our problems in a federal service.

It is embarrassingly obvious that government needs to be respected as a career among the general public and among businessmen as well as within government itself. It should carry with it dignity and honor. Such respect is dependent upon two main factors: effective, efficient, and honest operation by government; and the understanding of the objectives and conditions of government operation by those outside government. The first of these factors is not hard to attain with good men. The second calls for the best attention of our educators and leaders toward the creation of a tradition of individual responsibility among all of us. I don't believe that the university's task is accomplished by providing specially trained men for service in government. This will, of course, help. What is really needed, in my opinion, is far greater emphasis in our educational system as a whole, and especially in our universities, on the preparation of students for responsible citizenship, both *inside* and *outside* government. If that can be done, all the rest will follow.

6

PROBLEMS OF STRUCTURE
AND PERSONNEL

BY H. STRUVE HENSEL

THE administrative management of a modern democracy, such as the United States, is far from a simple matter. Such a nation has developed into an extended complex organism, deeply concerned with the detailed mechanics of supervising at many levels the living conditions for great masses of people under varying circumstances. The size and scope of its activities almost defy description. The days when a prospective governmental administrator could confidently approach his job with a smattering of political philosophy and a bit of bookkeeping knowledge are gone forever. Today his problems run the gamut of taxation, labor, agriculture, sanitation, finance, mining, housing, domestic and foreign trade of all kinds, transportation, and national security in a scientific wonder world. Furthermore, that is only a partial list of the activities which must be dealt with and coordinated. An organizational chart of our administrative side of government would confuse nearly anyone. Business experience, without something more, is not the complete training for such a job. There is as yet no single business enterprise in our country which even approaches the intricacies of modern government. Consequently, a realization of the tremendous size and complexity of the administrative problem is the obvious starting point for any consideration of the problems of top management in government.

There is another complicating factor in governmental administration which has no precise parallel in business. That is the direct responsibility of the administrator to that surging mass known as "the public." The corporate executive is, of course, responsible to his company's stockholders. That, however, is a comparatively limited group and there are many legal and natural circumstances which restrict the extent to which stockholders can question and interfere with corporate executives. The sky, however, is the limit with respect to the public and its servants. Public accountability of the governmental administrator is a night and day affair. He is bombarded with letters of criticism and demand. His administration is investigated publicly and privately. The people's representatives in Congress seem tireless in the pursuit of the administrator. It is impossible to please all of the congressmen at any time. In addition, there are the self-appointed investigators, the commentators, columnists, and private scandal seekers. Each one has a special angle and the newspapers seem to prefer stories of mistake and disagreement. Worst of all, the public is most fickle and changeable. Administrative programs and procedures which ignore the possible desires of the public or, to use more dignified language, the political implications, cannot hope to succeed, irrespective of soundness in logic or economics.

The influence of the investigating committee and the dissatisfied congressman is not always generally appreciated. It often far exceeds the popular support of such activities. Often it is necessary to yield in spite of a contrary belief just to prevent undue interference with smooth execution. The lash of this investigatory whip is felt by everyone in government. Consequently, the governmental administrator must have more than his share of tact and patience. Those who have purposely or inadvertently made government their career develop a somewhat calloused hide. Nevertheless, they do not escape being influenced by this phenomenon. The businessman, who ventures into government in times of crisis and for particular purposes, is often more sensitive, and this irritant, perhaps inherent in the maintenance of democratic control, undoubtedly does much to discourage the flow of able men into government. Consequently, government, which needs the best talent available, is often forced to accept the more mediocre administrator, because many of the better men refuse to submit to such attacks.

In the light of such general background, the basic problems of governmental administration may be classified into two major categories. First, there are the problems of structural organization and coordination. Second, there are the problems of staffing the offices and agencies with personnel able to function efficiently and harmoniously.

A discussion of radical changes in the structural organization of our government would not be too helpful. If any changes can or should be made, they will have to be gradual and will develop slowly over many years. We are too accustomed to the basic organizational form to make any sudden and extensive changes. Evolution in that respect will always be preferred to revolution. The size and complexity of modern government can hardly be substantially reduced. We will do well to maintain the status quo. Perhaps, in time, the federal government may be persuaded to withdraw from some of the fields entered during and before the war and some problems now dealt with on a national basis may be turned over to local execution and control. Our government, however, will remain big—and its activities will continue to spread out over all phases of our national life.

By such conclusion it is not meant that nothing can be done in respect of further simplification and improved coordination. Much must be done in both of those fields. The cost of government has become far too great and the lack of effective coordination has been obvious for some time. We have achieved vitality and dynamism at the expense of smoothness and economy. The need for better coordination of governmental activities has been dramatized in the discussions about the reorganization of the armed services. The problem is, however, not peculiar to the army, navy, or the air force. It exists with respect to every executive department and with respect to the over-all relationship between the executive and legislative. It is one of the major—if not the outstanding—unsolved problems of modern administrative organization. The unfortunate dilemma is that increased coordination seems always to involve expense.

Additional arrangements to improve coordination, such as a permanent presidential secretariat to assist the Cabinet, a strengthened Bureau of the Budget, an improved General Accounting Office, and special liaison or coordinating bodies, have often been suggested. It may even be that, by more comprehensive liaison between the executive departments and the legislative bodies, much can be done to temper irresponsible criticism of public servants. All of such changes are worth careful consideration.

Nevertheless, it is my opinion that the basic need of top management in government is improved personnel. The streamlined organizational chart accomplishes nothing by itself. Books of rules and outlines of policies, no matter how inspired, have little effectiveness unless administered by capable human beings. Sometimes poorly conceived organizations operate efficiently as a result of extraordinary personnel and, on the other hand, the most scientifically designed structures fail because of a lack of adequate personnel. Such occurrences often lead to the erroneous theory that organizational forms can be entirely ignored. While I do not subscribe to that doctrine, it is my belief that a substantial improvement in our managerial personnel would produce a tremendous lift in administration with very few structural changes.

It may, for instance, be that the necessary coordination of activities will be achieved more through improved and more permanent personnel than through organizational changes. That, I believe, has been the British experience. Much has been written and said about the British skill in coordinating an equally widely flung governmental administration. Many of such laudatory statements are true. I have not been able to discover any particularly inspired organizational pattern in the British government to which such results can be fairly attributed. It seems to me that the British coordination is brought about not so much by the Council for Imperial Defence or any of its successors, the newly created Defence Committee, or the Cabinet Secretariat, but rather by the character, training, and permanence of the top British civil servants. The staffs of those specially designed coordinating organizations are too small in number to keep their fingers on every push button. Their activities are clearly restricted by the hours in a day and the endurance of the human mind and body.

The career servants in the administrative class of the British civil service are devoted to coordination. As a result of their common experience and training, they think and act in harmony. As a matter of fact, it might almost be said that they think, act, dress, and look alike. That group numbers approximately 2,000 men. They are spread through all the agencies of government and it is that class which supplies the men for the top administrative jobs in the British government. The top positions comparable to our under secretaries and assistant secretaries are filled by those career men, as well as the lower administrative positions. Also the men in this class are often shifted from department to department, and in the aggregate such a body of men possesses a comprehensive knowledge of British governmental administration. They worship at the altar of coordination and the job is well done.

The civil service group in the United States makes no pretense of supplying the men for top management positions. The ceiling for our civil servants is the directorship of a division or branch in the generalist class and a few top specialist jobs, such as general counsel to a department, chief engineer, and some scientific positions. No effort is made to train our civil servants for the top generalist positions. Since more rapid promotion is achieved in the specialist classes, the better men are attracted into those fields. Under secretaries and assistant secretaries, except for one assistant secretary position in the treasury and a few isolated instances during the war, are filled from private life. The tenure of office of such men is extremely short and the normal administrative principle of promotion through the ranks to the top jobs is not followed. They seldom know each other or much about the job before appointment.

As a matter of fact, our whole approach to the top administrative positions is rather curious. The secretary of a department is usually thought to be a combination of three men in one. Since he is automatically in the President's Cabinet, he should be a wise political adviser to the President. Since he is also the head of a huge governmental department, he is expected to be a competent top administrator. Unfortunately, in our political system, he is also required to be a man deserving of political reward. Marked preeminence in one or two of such fields is sometimes found in a single man, but the perfect three-in-one combination is almost an impossibility. The under secretaries and assistant secretaries, although supposedly filling purely administrative jobs, are frequently chosen for political reasons or because, in private life, they have won the confidence of the secretary. Administrative experience within the government is not usually the qualifying requirement. Although we would be thoroughly surprised if a corporation should follow that procedure in respect to its executive officers, we are quite complacent about that procedure in the more difficult job of governmental administration. It is a wonder to me that our administration functions as well as it does.

If we so desired, a permanent career service equivalent in quality to the British administrative class could be produced in the United States. In fact, all that is necessary is sufficient desire and the lapse of time necessary for the new group to work their way to the top. In the meantime, there are a number of competent men in the civil service who could serve in the top jobs with distinction. Such permanent career service, to be attractive, would require more adequate pay for the top jobs and for some of the intermediate positions, increased public respect, full opportunity for promotion according to merit, security, and adequate training, both in our universities and in the earlier years of government service.

The necessary increased pay would not be unduly expensive. Governmental pay need never be fixed at a level competitive with business. While security and a decent standard of living is important for a government servant and his family, there are many compensations other than money which attract the public executive. Even under our present system, the scope of his day-to-day problems provides a stimulation and inspiration not obtainable in private life. There is a continuous challenge in the unceasing problems and a real lift through the realization that his decisions frequently affect every fiber of our country's life. Even with present low pay, men who have tasted the heady cup of government often stay at that fountain, in spite of a reduced ability to provide for the future of their families.

The top pay to which the British administrative civil servant aspires is £3,500. Upon retirement, he receives an annuity computed by multiplying an average of his last three years pay by the fraction of the number of years served over the denominator of 80. In addition, the retired servant is given a tax-free lump sum payment on retirement, equivalent to three times the amount of his annuity. If a man enters the service, as is anticipated, at twenty years of age and serves his expected forty years, he is retired at sixty-two on half pay. If he has achieved the top salary of £3,500, he receives a tax-free lump sum payment of £5,250 and an annuity for the rest of his life of £1,750. Not all men achieve that result, but the path is always open for such achievement through demonstrated ability.

A similar arrangement in the United States, allowing for the difference in price levels by valuing the English pound at $5, would probably require a top pay of $17,500. Such a man would receive a tax-free lump sum retirement payment of $25,000 and annual retired pay of $8,750 per annum. On such pay, a man would never become rich but he would be assured of decent living. The tax-free feature of the lump sum payment on retirement is most important, and the graduated attainment of that endowment payment through accumulated years of service tends to hold in the government service many men who might otherwise be attracted into business. If efficient top management could be achieved at that price, it would be extremely cheap.

If, to such pay, could be added increased public recognition of the dignity and importance of public service (which might involve a new system of public honors and medals), I have no doubt that our government could successfully compete with industry, commerce, and the professions for the best talent in our country.

Young men, upon leaving college, choose their vocations for reasons other than a search for the maximum financial rewards. A certain percentage of our best university and technical school graduates always goes into professions such as the ministry, medicine, and teaching, which do not promise the same financial rewards as commerce and trade. The British experience has been that their administrative service is classified as a respected profession and I am sure the same result would obtain in this country. Once competent men are attracted on a career basis, the financial achievement depends on training and a fair promotion system.

Our present system militates against permanent careers and provides no procedure for entrance at the bottom and regular progression to the top. Outstanding men who may be appointed to the positions of under secretary or assistant secretary have no option to make such jobs their permanent careers. An under secretary or assistant secretary cannot decide whether he will leave. He can decide only when. Except for the foreign service under the supervision of the Department of

State, a young man cannot enter the government service in a position which will assure training, promotion, and security. I can remember that defect being dramatized by five young naval officers of unusual ability, who proffered themselves at the end of the war as raw material for permanent governmental careers. They were all college graduates and had distinguished themselves in the navy and the marine corps during the war. They were willing to make government their career if they could be assured of training and opportunity. After considerable search, all of these men abandoned the idea. There was no place for them in our approach to administration.

The major objection to the British system is that it produces a closed career service, i.e. unless a man enters the administrative class at the bottom at the age of twenty to twenty-two years, he can never serve his government in that capacity. That fault has been recognized and the British are working on a plan to eliminate that defect. The threat of a closed career service could, however, be easily avoided by allowing exceptional men to enter the service at varying levels. It is not an insurmountable obstacle. Through such a career group there could well be provided skill in administration, continuity of management, and a high degree of coordination. The business of government could go on without the present hazards of continuous turnover of personnel and the long period of indecision while the executive is learning his job. On the debit side of the ledger there is the risk of stereotyped thinking, delays through adherence to precedent, and some loss of vitality through the elimination of frequent changes in personnel. Many of such disadvantages would, however, be alleviated greatly by the introduction of outstanding men at grades higher than the entrance grade. On balance, it is my belief that the advantages would far outweigh the disadvantages.

In spite of that conclusion, there is serious question whether such solution of our problem would be satisfactory in the United States. I am very doubtful whether our people would accept a permanent administrative group secure from reprisals at the polls. Yet unless such career service is safe from party reversals, the desired standard of ability would not be attracted and continuity would not be possible. It is unfortunate that the British distinction between political policies and governmental administration has never been recognized in the United States. When a political party is turned out of office we insist on making a clean sweep. Furthermore, our elections are frequently decided not so much by positive votes for a political party but rather by negative votes against the other party. If that deep-seated American political emotion cannot be eliminated—and I fear it cannot—the career administrative service, in spite of its many advantages, will not work. Successful administration in government must above all satisfy and please the people.

If my fears are shared generally, the idea of a career service must be forgotten. Yet the problem does not vanish so easily. Top flight men must still be attracted into the government service if our administration is to meet our needs.

There is, in my opinion, only one alternative solution. The successful business and professional men in our country could be educated to serve some period of their lives in the governmental service. Such service could become a hallmark of success. The necessity of more adequate pay and increased public respect will be the same, if satisfactory men are to be attracted. Such men could rotate through the government service and, even if the periods of service for each man are comparatively short, many advantages will accrue which are not inherent in the current system. The government will be energized by the continuous injection of new thoughts and fresh vitality. Over a period of years, business and government will become mutually educated as to their respective problems. The businessmen serving in the government will not only bring back new and different ideas as to the reasons for certain types of governmental action, but they will leave in all brackets of the governmental service some knowledge of the needs and problems of business and industry. In time, the present stone wall between government and business should be completely demolished. Continuity of management and coordination through a large permanent group of administrators will not be provided by this program. That will be unfortunate, and yet other methods may be found for remedying that defect. Increased dynamism will be a fair price to pay for the failure to assure smoothness and continuity.

The basic question in this suggestion is whether our business and professional men can be persuaded to serve a period of time in the government. Based on past experience, the chances are not of the best. Except for the war, the customary attitude of business and the professions has been to regard government as a separate entity, completely set apart from their everyday life. Successful men are inclined to view the government service as an inferior endeavor, to be taken up by second grade men who cannot achieve success elsewhere. Such attitudes are, of course, erroneous and must bear a large share of the blame for inefficient governmental administration. Nevertheless, it exists, and considerable education will be necessary to make our business and professional men aware of their responsibility for providing good men for government. Nothing is solved by vehement condemnations at the luncheon table. The men in government are doing the best they know. The mistakes result from a lack of better men to direct them —and that supply is hoarded by our various corporations and firms. Yet efficient governmental administration contributes directly, not only to increased public welfare but to the long term prospects of our business and professional activities. Quite aside from aiding general welfare, the business and professional men who try a turn at government service will be helping themselves to the greatest extent possible. I still cling to the hope that the soundness of such conclusions will penetrate the consciousness of all.

Structure and Personnel

There is a third possibility, which is a compromise between the two approaches. It is the establishment of a limited career service—buttressed by the creation of one permanent administrative position in each department or agency, with the title and rank of under secretary or assistant secretary, to which only civil servants shall be eligible. Since such career service will be small, it might be more readily accepted by our people than the allocation of all under secretary and assistant secretary positions to a career service. The opportunity for improved administration is also restricted under this plan. I doubt whether sufficient top management positions would be created to attract an adequate supply of good men. The suggestion might, however, be worth trying, in order to explore the attitude of the American people toward a career service. If the plan should prove acceptable, it might well be expanded into covering a larger number of administrative positions.

Irrespective of the program adopted, there is a distinct need for more attention to the type of education which accelerates and assures the satisfactory development of the generalist administrator. We clearly suffer from too many specialists. The British theory has been to insist on a more or less classical education for their administrative class. They believe that the classics provide the best mental training for comprehensive understanding and leadership. Whether this country would agree with the British dogma is doubtful. I am definitely inclined to question it. It seems to me that some factual knowledge of our modern world—economics and the social sciences—although not to the extent required for a specialized profession, is essential properly to equip the effective administrator. While courses in public accounting, farm problems, sanitation, and the like clearly do not provide the proper mental arsenal for the generalist, there is little doubt but that a man would prove a better government servant if he is given an understanding of at least the basic governmental problems. Probably these observations should not be limited to the governmental generalist. There would seem to be little distinction between the education necessary and desirable for the top flight governmental servant and for the man who expects to take a leading position in private life. The educational problem, therefore, seems not to involve special preparation for government service, but rather the assurance of education which clearly prepares our young men for leadership and influence in the present world.

The achievement of improved governmental management has a better chance today than ever before. In spite of the defects in our system, a good job was accomplished during the war. The men who came into the government service from various private pursuits attained a high degree of success. Our war record in administration was high. I am not willing to bow to any one. Our inefficiences were more than balanced by dynamism and force. Comparatively little remains to be accomplished if we can sustain the patriotism and spirit of the war. Furthermore, this country now possesses a larger group than ever before of men interested in public service. The need for good governmental administration is generally recognized and the responsibility of every citizen for achieving the desired result is increasingly recognized. We have a sound foundation upon which we can easily build, if we are willing to insist that we now struggle through the uncertainties and difficulties to a definitive decision.

PART III

THE PERSONNEL NEEDS IN THE
INTERNATIONAL FIELD

7

THE NEEDS OF THE FOREIGN SERVICE

BY GEORGE F. KENNAN

IN A series of lectures which he delivered some years ago before the French Academy, the celebrated French diplomat, Monsieur Jules Cambon, made this statement: "Democracies," he said, "will always have diplomacy; it is a question whether they will ever have diplomats." M. Cambon pointed out that the profession of diplomacy demanded of its devotees *une certaine habitude du monde*, in other words a touch of worldly wisdom and sophistication which, he said, would always be suspect in the robust society of a democratic state. The average man, he felt, would always wish to be represented by someone very much like himself, and he would look with suspicion and hostility on anyone who had acquired a *habitude du monde* which he himself did not share.

Many times in the course of two decades in the foreign service, I have had occasion to ponder those words of Jules Cambon. Sometimes, when the circumstances of life were particularly unpleasant, and especially on occasions when I had been forced to demand from officers on my own staff more than I thought men should normally be asked to give, it has made me rather bitter to read in the papers from home the faded cracks about our "white-spatted, cookie-pushing diplomats"; and I wondered whether perhaps M. Cambon was not right after all in his skepticism about the willingness of democracies to be represented by people rendered competent by background and training for their jobs.

M. Cambon's premise that the profession of diplomacy requires personal qualities and a personal balance beyond the average remains, I think, unchallengeable; and one of the basic problems in foreign service training is to find out by what means these qualities can be appropriately instilled.

As I think back over the hundreds of foreign service officers I have known and over the experiences they have had in the service, it seems to me that the worst of the personal failures have arisen from deficiencies of character. They have been the result of an inability of the man to adjust himself to the peculiar and often complicated demands of a foreign environment. Sometimes it has been an inability to cope with the variety and potency of the beverages which cross one's path in appalling profusion in the course of a diplomatic career; sometimes it has been the variety—and I almost said the potency—of the ladies who appear in only slightly less abundance. Again, very often, even when the officer might alone have been able to contend successfully with the problems of life abroad, he has not been able to choose a wife of whom the same thing might be said or he has not been able to bring her to an understanding of the part she must play in his work. For in this modern world there are few professions where the efforts of husband and wife must be so closely fused toward a common objective as in the profession of diplomacy.

It is a primary requirement for the successful foreign service officer that he be an emotionally robust individual: sensitive enough and thoughtful enough to avoid the bumptious obtuseness that sometimes goes with extroversion; yet not too deeply concentrated on himself and his own problems; imbued with an interest in and a liking for people, and a healthy curiosity for all that goes on about him; and capable of enjoying all the amenities of life in a foreign community without becoming beholden to any of them. For this we need men with a reasonable harmony of mental, physical, and emotional development, men with a strong sense of obligation and loyalty to whatever group they are associated with, and above all men with a sound American sense of humor, capable of recognizing and contemplating some of the sorry realities of the world in which we live without being plunged into overly tragic depths of gloom and despair.

I do not wish to imply that it is primarily the job of the universities to produce character for the foreign service. Much of the task of character-building is admittedly removed from their competence. I am skeptical about special techniques for building character. It is my own belief that the qualities which render a man personally fit for the profession of diplomacy are ones engendered mainly in the home, and at a relatively early age. But the university can at least keep a watchful eye on students who are heading in the direction of diplomacy, and it can warn—or refrain from encouraging—people who, however brilliant, show marked signs of emotional immaturity or instability and who do not bid fair to react with reasonable resilience to "the slings and arrows of outrageous fortune" with which a diplomatic career is bound to be replete.

This is not going to be an easy task. Appearances are deceiving. Too often it is the man who in his college years basks in the sunlight of athletic success and student popularity who later wilts under the loneliness and frustration of life abroad. Sometimes it is the moody, unadjusted student, struggling to forge his own standards in a callous collegiate society, who develops within himself the thoughtfulness to comprehend a foreign environment and the self-discipline to adjust himself to it. There is a highly crucial area between the slow development which often goes with real promise and the shallow precociousness which can gleam so brightly in men of college age. We are dealing here with subtleties of personality which in my opinion surpass the scientific approach and which call for that fifth sense of human understanding which has always been the signal gift of great teachers everywhere.

But if deficiencies of character account for the worst catastrophes in the career of foreign service people, deficiencies of education probably account for the relatively high percentage of official mediocrity; i.e. for the failure of so many men to at-

tain more than a very limited value to the service. It is to education that we must look to increase the percentage of officers
in the service who will be regarded as outstanding people
wherever they function and who can be relied upon to undertake the most responsible jobs. This is, of course, where academic training comes into its own.

It is my own belief that full success in foreign service, and by
that I mean the attainment of really high value to the government, requires an educational background considerably wider
than what is afforded by the normal undergraduate training.
A successful representative abroad should be not only better
educated than this training affords with respect to the world
outside the borders of the United States but he should also have
an exceptional understanding of his own country. He should
be better equipped than is the average American college graduate in all those things which contribute to his ability to observe
and interpret a foreign environment, in the things that appeal
to the eye and the ear: architecture, applied arts, industrial
processes, methods of agriculture—in all those things, in other
words, that make up the outward expressions of custom, tradition, and belief. (I have often been appalled and dismayed to
see the imperviousness and indifference of young Americans to
phenomena of a foreign environment which are new to them
and which, as it now seems to me, should set them agog with
astonishment and wonder. And what appalls and dismays me
most is to reflect that of all the Americans I have known of
whom this might be said, I think the worst case I have ever
known was myself, as I was when I first went to live abroad
some twenty-five years ago.) Finally, the aspirant to the foreign service should have sufficient experience with real scholarship, in the genuine academic sense, to understand at least the
meaning of that concept, and to distinguish an unscholarly
and unsound bit of intellectual work from a scholarly and
sound one. I personally do not think we can say that average

undergraduate training in this country generally satisfies these demands.

It was for this reason that I was one of those who looked with some favor on the scheme of a special Foreign Service Academy along the lines of West Point and Annapolis, for it seemed to me that with a greater concentration of effort, with the elimination of many of the nonessentials that go with normal American college life (nonessentials at least from our foreign service standpoint) and with a stricter and clearer concept of purpose throughout the institution, perhaps we might hope to come closer to the standards I have just outlined, without prolonging the actual term of study.

That possibility has been rejected, and there are indeed weighty factors which militate against it. But we are still faced with the problem which it was designed to meet.

Again we have the possibilities of in-service training. I am enthusiastic about that program. I think it deserves every support. But I am still inclined to feel that the raw material with which we work in the service should come to us initially with broader and better intellectual equipment than has been the case in the past. And this, to my mind, means that a larger percentage of our candidates should undergo a year or two of appropriate postgraduate study before coming to the foreign service.

Here there arises the inevitable question as to what sort of postgraduate training is appropriate. In my opinion, the subject of postgraduate study is not really important, providing it affords a genuine intellectual discipline and the appreciation of the meaning of scholarship which I have just mentioned. Here, of course, we have the question of special instruction in the foreign relations field. This is a very complicated one. There is no simple answer to it. My own feeling is that where such instruction is founded on a fearless realism as to the nature of the world in which we live and particularly the nature and limitations of our own country, and where it is rooted firmly in the basic sciences (of which it can, in my opinion, constitute only an eclectic synthesis), then it can be possibly the best preparation a man could have for foreign service. But where foreign affairs instruction fails to meet these requirements, where it is not based on realism, and where people become carried away with the pleasant sound of their own pleasant words, then I think it can easily degenerate into a pseudo-science, which is of little use to anybody and particularly to us. What is of primary importance is the discipline and appreciation of scholarship which I have mentioned. What a foreign service officer needs is sufficient insight into one field of academic research to enable the man to understand the intertwining and the interdependence of all forms of human learning, to give in this way a universal quality to his curiosity and his interests, and to instill in him a dignified humility before the complexity and profundity of the problems of our time. Any study that accomplishes this purpose will give a man a power impetus on the road to success in a diplomatic career.

Now it may be argued that to encourage prior postgraduate training of candidates for the service would give an edge to the wealthier students and to graduates of the older and wealthier institutions of the east, and that in this way it would serve to disrupt the wide geographical background of the service and to lay it open again to the charges of eastern cliquishness to which it has so often been subjected in the past. There are two things, I think, to be said about this. In the first place I do not think that it is necessarily true. I am sure that the type of postgraduate training I have in mind can be and is being found all over this country. But in the second place I think we should be wary of the pitfalls of this question of sectionalism. I agree heartily that the broader the base of our service geographically and the more representative its members can be of all classes and sections of the American public the better. I earnestly hope that the development of academic facilities and the use made of them will be so evenly distributed throughout the country that a natural selection of men, by aptitude for this life and this work, will automatically prove to be a geographically representative one. But I hope that we will not make a fetish of our desire to spread the base of the service. I see no reason why we should curtail in any way the qualitative standards of the service out of apprehension of what may be said by a few outside critics. I think we should take good men wherever we can find them. I think this principle should lead to a healthy competition between the various sections of the country and if Massachusetts, for example, fails to furnish its quota of likely candidates then, I say, so much the worse for Massachusetts.

Now these are only two points of many which could be mentioned. But they may give an idea of what some of us in the field would like the man to be who comes to us as the budding foreign service officer. We want him to continue to be a gentleman,. as he has been in the past. We would prefer to see him somewhat more of a scholar, perhaps, than he has been in the past. And if, in addition to that, he can also contrive to be not only a good judge of whisky but a discriminating connoisseur of all those delicate and sometimes dangerous amenities which do so much (more than some of us realize) to make diplomatic intercourse possible and effective, then I think it will truly be possible to say the universities of this country have done all in their power to assure the adequacy of our foreign service, as an instrument of state policy.

8

TRAINING FOR THE FOREIGN SERVICE

BY SELDEN CHAPIN

WHAT should an American diplomat be? I know there is no single answer to that question, but I will venture a hypothesis merely to preface these remarks. I believe he should be a man of broad humanism, manifesting some of the best typical aspects of the American culture, capable of understanding at least one other area and civilization, competent in the analysis of modern society, and a gentleman. Before you shy away at that last archaic word, I hasten to add that I define it as meaning simply a good human being.

Diplomats, nevertheless, have always been "fixers." Indeed the ancient commentators like De Mothe, Le Vayer and Vera de Cuniga date the beginnings of the institution from the opening of Pandora's box—it seems that we have been trying to put the lid back on ever since.

In his book *Diplomacy*, Harold Nicholson, himself a diplomat, and a son of a great British permanent Under Secretary of State, concentrates on the qualities of character, or what he calls the seven diplomatic virtues: truthfulness, precision, calm, good temper, patience, modesty, and loyalty; he concedes that a reader may object that he has forgotten intelligence, knowledge, discernment, prudence, hospitality, charm, industry, courage, and tact; but he replies that these are taken for granted. I go a little further than Nicholson and take the whole catalogue for granted. And I would add that he must have an insatiable curiosity about everything that goes on about him. I trust that our diplomats will be men of character and possessed of the "moral influence" which M. Jules Cambon described as the most essential qualification; but I do not believe that this essay can measure the character-building potential of our educational institutions, and I believe our concern is more with the intellectual formation the new foreign service officer is to receive.

To begin with, it is a *new* diplomacy for which he must be trained. His service will be very different from that in the past, not only because his work will be of more vital concern to the nation in winning and maintaining the peace, but also because he will have to perform new work of a specialized character under different conditions. During the war, officials of executive departments frequently entered into direct contact with their opposite numbers abroad. The myriad Allied combined boards for supply and shipping, lend-lease, economic warfare, finance, and intelligence drew diplomacy out of the chancery into new adventures.

A professional foreign service under these conditions must be able to contribute something more to the conduct of foreign relations than efficient secretariats and the rituals of old school-tie diplomacy. It must know the substance of the specialized work which the specialists are called upon to perform and must be equipped either to participate directly in such activities or to assist, guide, and coordinate them. If it cannot, a country impatient of dilettantism and worshipful of the expert may decide that it is superfluous. It may well continue as a distinguished relic of the nineteenth century, but the peculiar contribution it has to make in "know-how," in discipline and continuity, in the arts of negotiation will go for naught.

New tasks mean new problems for the foreign service. In the field of economics for example, the foreign service officer will be doing things quite different from the trade promotion of the past. Instead of the weapons in the ingenious arsenal of economic warfare, he will be using peacetime tools, in aid of the American economy, as safeguards against future wars, and as factors to bring about a more equitable distribution of the world's goods. As one of our officers has suggested, "some of the trade intelligence methods learned during the war, which do not depend on sources and procedures appropriate only to warfare, will become part of peacetime practice. The experience gained by evaluating the economic position of an entire country by a few hundred new techniques will help to open new horizons to the foreign service officer." And American business will be the direct beneficiary.

It was Canning whose audacious theory that public opinion should actually be invoked in the councils of diplomacy caused Metternich to describe him as a "malevolent meteor hurled by divine providence on Europe." The power of public opinion has grown mightily from Canning's day to that of our new information service. Today relations between states are increasingly relations between peoples rather than between governments. The foreign service officer will have to combine this force with diplomacy and he will need to participate in the activities of the cultural and informational agencies.

Our foreign policy is bound to involve a relatively large United States force in being whether solely for national defense or as contingent commitments under the United Nations Security Council. In the future, the foreign service officer must know more about our military and naval establishment and its policies.

I have said enough, I believe, to show why the foreign service must be organized and staffed somewhat differently from that of the past.

In order to give you some idea of the service which is being built for the new diplomacy, I should like to summarize briefly some of the changes made in our Foreign Service Act by the new act of 1946 (Public Law 74–79th Congress). This act provides for the first major reorganization of the service since the Rogers Act of 1924 which merged the diplomatic and consular services into our present foreign service. The draft passed by Congress is based upon the following principles: The concept of a career service remains paramount; political influence will be excluded, while compensation should be sufficient to attract able men regardless of the possession of private means. A disciplined and mobile corps of trained men should be maintained through entry at the bottom on the basis of competitive examination and advancement by merit to positions of command.

"At the same time," to quote a report on the act by the House Committee on Foreign Affairs, "any service which overdevelops self-sufficiency, and evaluates its performance by criteria peculiar to itself, belies its name. The professional instrument established by this bill must be flexible. It must be responsive to the constantly changing needs of government. To achieve this, there should be provision for inter-departmental consultation on the administration of the Service; especially qualified persons from elsewhere should be brought into the Service for temporary periods and have the status of Foreign Service Officers; outstanding men should be able to join the permanent service at ranks commensurate with their age and qualifications but not in such numbers as to nullify the career principle; and there should be a corps of administrative and technical experts to bring continuity and expert knowledge to the maintenance of the Service."

To carry out these purposes the new act provides for the establishment of three branches of the service; it is obvious that the training problem will be different for each branch.

The three branches may be briefly defined as line, staff, and reserve. The first-named group will be the permanent professional service of which the nucleus will be the present career foreign service. This group will, we hope, furnish the men who rise to positions of command as chiefs of missions and important officers in the Department of State; they will be chosen by one of the most rigorous competitive examinations we are able to devise and will be subject to certain conditions of discipline not common to the other branches; promotion will be by an adaptation of the navy's selection-out system whereunder men who fail to win promotion in a given period of time are eliminated from the service; this group will also be considerably more mobile than the other groups and the obligation to go to any post at any time is implicit in the commissions given to its members. This group might be compared to the "line" of the navy. We shall, however, see to it that this "line" branch includes a heavy proportion of specialized talents. There are already within the service brains and aptitudes for most of the special tasks of the present era, provided only that the department gives adequate training and opportunity to these skills. This we plan to do by our system of "in-service" training, and it is just here that I believe the university and the department, working together, can achieve the best results.

The staff branch will include all other American employees of the service. It will include all personnel formerly in the administrative, fiscal, and clerical services, in our wartime auxiliary foreign service, and will include specialists whose work will be of long tenure as compared to those in the reserve, or which is generally of a lesser order of responsibility. Generally speaking, the group will correspond to the CAF classification of the civil service. The training program for this group is twofold; in the lower ranks it will chiefly be comprised of foreign service and area orientation, including language, but for the higher grades of specialists we plan some "in-service" training to develop specialties.

The third group, that is, the reserve group, will make it possible for us to call on the best talents in the country for periods of temporary work with the foreign service; men will enter as foreign service reserve officers from elsewhere in government or from private life. While some of these people will have general duties, most will be taken on to perform very special tasks; for example, a study of metallurgy behind the Urals, or of malarial control in the Nile Delta, or of the geology of the Arabian peninsula. A number of the specialists remaining from our wartime auxiliary will go into this branch, and it is here that we expect to put many of the specialists from the writing, editing, and research fields which Assistant Secretary Benton proposes to recruit in the informational and cultural program. Obviously the training program for the reserves will be primarily one of orientation in the foreign service, or perhaps an accelerated language brush-up rather than work in the specialties they have already acquired.

In our 1948 budget estimates we asked Congress for 1,500 foreign service officers (as compared to about 950 for the previous year); 687 reserve officers, and 1,090 staff officers and employees. To complete this picture as to the quantity and deployment of our personnel, I should point out that recruitment for the bottom ranks of the foreign service is now limited to veterans. By 1947 we planned to take in, by a series of three special examinations, some 400 young veterans of the recent war; also, as a companion piece to the Foreign Service Act of 1946, we have a special manpower law which will enable us to take into the service in the near future in the middle and upper ranks up to 250 exceptionally qualified persons who have had either a year and a half of government experience or whose military experience appears to the examiners to fit them for the service.

I hope that I have said enough to describe the new service for which men must be trained and to make clear its administrative divisions. I should like now to pass to the training program and to begin with the level of undergraduate training. It is clear that we must mobilize for the foreign service the very best brains and character in each generation and train them at a markedly higher level of requirement and in a much more serious and impressive manner than was ever reached in the comparatively easy circumstances of the past. Our opinion is that, beyond orientation and indoctrination, a kind of "in-service" training must be continued through a foreign service officer's career both for the sake of efficiency and to sustain morale. We believe that this instruction should be at the graduate and not the undergraduate level. We believe that the best basic equipment for the foreign service and those personal qualities desirable in an American diplomat are best acquired or brought out by experience in established American schools and colleges, rather than by training in a special "trade" school, or in a diplomatic institution patterned on West Point or Annapolis. It is true that an opposing view is rather widely held but I think this proceeds from a general feeling that some special training is necessary rather than from an enlightened consideration of the levels at which it should be applied. Even so, a few of our ablest diplomats have become so impressed with the contentious nature of diplomacy today, that they would like to see the young bred to it in special schools, like Spartan children for the walls of Sparta.

The basic requirement of the American foreign service is a knowledge of the world and of man, of the ideas which belong to our time and of the roots from which these ideas have developed rather than a special technical education. An undergraduate foreign service academy would tend to stamp future foreign service officers in one mold, and might easily breed a caste spirit, the very thing that the department has sought to prevent by selecting men for the service from all segments of American life, as well as from diversified educational backgrounds and different sections of the country. In this connection, it is interesting to note that in 1941 when our last prewar public examinations were given, there were 440 candidates from 164 colleges and universities designated to take the examination. The 37 successful candidates represented 21 educational institutions and 14 states. In 1940, 483 candidates from 168 colleges and universities were designated for the examination. The 45 successful candidates represented 26 educational institutions and 18 states.

We are not satisfied, however, that we are drawing our recruits from the best levels in the colleges, and therefore we feel that a new and closer relation between the service and the colleges is necessary after the war. We are aware that the current of interest in foreign affairs is running more strongly in the universities than it ever has and we must seek a way to channel that interest to our advantage.

In the period from 1931 to 1941 we were recruiting a very good group for the service. I believe that the reasons for this were, first, a vastly improved type of examination developed under the leadership of Mr. Joseph C. Green, now executive director of our board of examiners and formerly of the department of history at Princeton; second, the depression, which enabled the service to compete successfully with private business in choosing good men; third, the gathering menace of the international situation which caused men of ability and vision to believe that they would find real opportunities and responsibilities in the foreign service; and fourth, increasing interest in the colleges in public service as a career. Except for the second point, all these factors are still active. Nevertheless, although we recruited and are still recruiting good men, I doubt if we are getting the best we could get or even that we are tapping the most likely "populations." There are many able men already in the professions, in business, and more recently in government who make a practice of steering good men into their offices. We have never had a similar "farm system" for the foreign service. Some of the abler and more audacious young men seem to prefer the freer operations and quicker promotions of business to enlisting in any hierarchical career services. Other reasons might be the supposed absence of a real job opportunity at the top in the foreign service which is suspected of being hidebound and clogged with petty jobs; the absence of opportunity for men with specialized talents or graduate training in a service built on a "Jack of all trades" concept; disinclination for service abroad, and lack of adequate foreign language training; and lastly, the feeling that to go into the service at all one has to have an independent income.

Of these factors, all can be counteracted in more or less degree by foreign service reforms; we can and are improving the promotion system; we are planning a staff branch which will have responsibility for many of the more routine assignments of the service; we have increased pay and opportunities, and in the future there should be no job in the service which a man cannot handle on his pay and allowances. We are threshing out the issue of greater area and regional specialization (and I hope it will end in better recognition of the specialists). We are providing "in-service" training which will make it possible for people to develop specialties, and we are bringing people home more often.

One gap which is still unplugged is a system of liaison with the universities so that they will send us better people and better trained people. We do not ask that universities prescribe courses for the foreign service oriented toward any particular "party line," but we would be very much interested in learning as much as we can about curricula designed for students in international affairs and in offering any suggestions we can. I do not want to go into types of courses or plans of study at this time, except to say that the area and regional programs now being offered by some colleges seem especially useful.

The trend seems to be away from the narrow conception of the social sciences, and I think this is to the good. It is true that we expect that most students will have worked in the field of the social sciences because this is the most appropriate context in which a candidate for the government service would acquire his education. Nevertheless, I should like to see the field widened enough so that men of intellectual distinction in fields not necessarily restricted to the social sciences would be encouraged to apply.

We welcome young men with specialized training in the field of international endeavor, but we welcome also the man with a good sound engineering education. Obviously we expect that all who will wish to enter the foreign service have an interest in foreign affairs. In fact, what we ask chiefly in the way of basic preparation for our candidates is a good broad education. We believe we can build on that and the proved capacity to grow intellectually.

In any case, we feel that in addition to the hard core of social sciences, languages, and civilizations, the applicant should be able to offer additional material. Few men have made a choice of life work in their junior year in college, nor has the average junior necessarily hit upon the best field of concentration for his interests and abilities. Let us suppose that he has followed a course consisting of a major in philosophy with minors in medieval and American history. The present examinations, designed to match the usual preparation, would tap his scholastic experiences at only one or two points; yet it is entirely conceivable that he has as sound a basis for social studies and for practicing diplomacy as a man who has spent most of his time reading in modern history and current economics.

We recommend, therefore, that preparation for the service should, in the words of a report of the Harvard subcommittee on languages and international affairs of the Committee on Educational Policy, "bring the individual social sciences, and the social sciences and the humanities into fruitful cooperation." We are investigating the possibility of revising our examination technique to make it possible for the candidate to offer a broader field of study than hitherto with some system of options as to subjects, like the British, which would ensure a reasonable concentration in the social sciences appropriate to a foreign service career while permitting other subjects to be included in the aggregate for which credit is given.

There is considerable difference of opinion among us in the department as to the next step. Should the student step immediately from the campus to the foreign service examination room? Or should he spend several years in graduate study or in business or government? It is true that some of our best officers are men who entered at relatively mature years, but on the other hand the qualities of youth—resilience and growth—are at a premium in these stressful years. Our best compromise is on age 25. This would allow the average student at least a year of graduate work, or an opportunity to acquire business experience which we would, as a general rule, recommend. We have under consideration, incidentally, decreasing the age range for entrance at the bottom to 21 to 31. It is now from 21 to 35. When older men enter the service, they will do so in restricted numbers elsewhere than at the bottom.

In the foreign service, specialization will begin after—rather than before—entry and some time after basic training is completed. This brings us to the subject of the Foreign Service Institute which will direct all programs of foreign service officers now recruited by a difficult competitive examination. These highly selected talents often atrophy even though there may be no lessening in the conscientious desire for self-improvement on the part of the individual. The reasons for this deterioration are to be sought in the manpower shortage prevailing since our suspension of recruitment after Pearl Harbor which makes it difficult to divert men to training assignments from the immediate task; in the absence of a rational assignment policy on the part of personnel management; and, most importantly, in the lack of a program of continuous training (like that which made our modern army) directed by a strong central authority which would keep men up-to-date in their specialties and in developments in American government and business. Accordingly, we planned the new institute to provide training at successive stages in an officer's career, comparable to that provided for army and navy officers in the command schools, and in the army and war colleges.

We have no intention of setting up a "government college" to offer feeble bureaucratic competition to established universities. In its higher echelons, the institute will administer comparatively little instruction on its own premises but will arrange for foreign service officers or departmental officers to work and consult at high levels, not only in the Department of State, but in any agency, in any business, research organization, or university where possibilities exist for widening the background of a governmental officer.

The institute, although closely affiliated with the department, and using classified material in its seminars, will nevertheless enjoy a certain autonomy. It should thus maintain sufficient academic prestige to attract a respectable staff.

In briefest outline the program of the institute would be the following. It will direct college liaison and will eventually have responsibility for devising examination techniques. In liaison with the Board of the Foreign Service it will attempt to validate these techniques with reference to performance in the service.

For foreign service officers and others going abroad it will provide orientation courses which will introduce newcomers to the new career, its organization, traditions, duties, standards, and describe briefly the position of the United States in world affairs, and teach the "tools" of the trade. During an officer's first field assignment, the institute will share responsibility for his training program, and assist in the evaluation of his work. At the end of the third and fourth year, the officer who survives the probationary stage will be brought to Washington for a year's training during which half of his time will be spent at the institute, the other half in the department, learning by doing.

The process of area specialization will commence at the beginning of this basic year. Thus, about half of the officers will elect or be designated to follow area studies while others will follow the "generalist" line. The specialist would be assigned to an area and spend the training time working on problems relating to the area. In order to develop his understanding of various aspects of the work of the department each officer will be rotated through four functional divisions. Morning courses at the institute will be integrated with the work done at the department. They should fall into one of two groups: general seminars pitched at a rather high theoretical level, and detailed and thorough courses in area specialization. For this instruction, the director will probably employ a panel of visiting professors appointed for one year, who may also act as consultants for various offices of the department.

In about the seventh or eighth year of the career, selected officers will attend specialized courses arranged by the institute. If the service accepts the responsibility for specialized work abroad, it must furnish special training to make its officers competent in new fields. In general the institute cannot give these courses itself, for it will not have a large enough staff. Therefore, it will act as educational broker arranging for officers to be sent to universities, colleges, research foundations, business companies, and other federal departments. This specialized work at the eighth year may possibly be followed by further work at a later stage in the career or by a general refresher course in economics, history, area civilizations or appropriate subjects, also in nongovernmental institutions. The extent to which this further program can be carried out will of course depend on the over-all work load of the service, the number of men we can afford to keep in training, and similar considerations. I am sure that you are all aware, that except for the army and navy, very few governmental departments have been able to sell a full time "in-training" program to Congress and the Bureau of the Budget.

The capstone of the training program would, of course, be the advanced course. Selected officers in the top ranks of the service would work under the guidance of the institute in collaboration with other specialists in foreign affairs in the preparation of long range reports upon major aspects of foreign policy. Such reports might very well find their way to the desk of the President, to the Cabinet and to the joint chiefs of staff.

In addition to this basic program for foreign service officers, the institute will direct various other courses, including important administrative, clerical, and office management programs and, as soon as and as rapidly as we can push it, an accelerated language program for all personnel. In addition to the language courses in Washington, we plan to have a number of field centers. We have begun the language work under the direction of Mr. Henry Lee Smith whose training in the linguistics field was received at Princeton and who had much to do with the accelerated techniques used in the armed forces. Our language program owes much to our consultation with the American Council of Learned Societies. I cannot stress too much the importance of this particular phase of the institute's program. Hitherto, ability has not been sufficiently emphasized in our service principally because typical Americans are not generally versed in languages and we wanted to recruit typical Americans. Now, however, the accelerated technique will make it possible for us to supply the deficiency. We hope that every foreign service officer (and his wife) will arrive at a new post equipped with at least fair fluency in the language of the country. He could not do an adequate job with less, especially in areas like much of Europe today where leaders and officials will, in most cases, come from the working, peasant, or middle classes and will speak only their native tongue.

Our beginnings are still rather modest. Our 1948 budget estimate was $603,681 which covered 72 faculty and administrative jobs, the costs of travel incident to the work of the institute, printing and binding expenses, contingent expenses, and the costs of instruction at universities. This last item breaks down into (1): $62,500 for the program of special language and area specialization of foreign service officers at American universities, including travel, tuition, and necessary materials; and (2) $25,000 for training of foreign service officers at graduate schools in other than language studies. With this sum we sent about ten officers, of from five to fifteen years of experience, to take general refresher courses in political, economic, and social studies, or to undertake specialized studies in fields in which a high level of professional competence is required.

Selden Chapin

At the same time the institute will carry on a really large program of orientation and language courses, and courses for secretarial and administrative personnel.

I imagine that many are most interested in the collaboration of the university and the department in graduate training and may be disappointed in the meagerness of our current program in this regard; we are presently curbed by both necessity and prudence. The institute must justify itself to a number of doubting Thomases in our own department and elsewhere by the utility of its vocational training and establish itself solidly before branching out. We do hope to expand the outside training project, from which I personally expect the greatest yield on our investment, as soon as our manpower deployment and our financial situation permit.

I would not presume to say much about the method of instruction which would be followed in these courses of graduate study, but I may indicate some limitations. I believe that we should start with one or two "pilot model" programs, both in area civilizations and in more general work.

I believe that the studies being made at Harvard, for instance, about which I have heard something from Dr. Pendleton Herring, present interesting possibilities. As he points out, most lecture courses would be quite inappropriate for the kind of students we expect to send to the universities. The best work would be done in seminars which would have the character of those governmental "working parties" with which foreign service officers are familiar. Such parties would work toward the goal of specific reports of findings on topics which have a particular relevance to the work of the foreign service. The instruction techniques might include some of the conference techniques of the School of Public Affairs at Princeton. I should like to emphasize, however, that the university should not be tempted too far into the vocational field. We do not need experts in shipping so much as we need well-rounded human beings. What our officers need from the university is that insight into causation and relation which comes from a leisured consideration of contemporary phenomena in the light of recorded experience. Such reflection is most fruitful when it combines in a single focus the outlook of a variety of scholars of the social sciences and the humanities. This approach appears to be that of the area and civilization programs now being constructed in many universities. Unfortunately it will be difficult for some time to come to spare officers for training assignments for more than a year at a time, so that some of the area programs would have to be condensed.

Our past experience in assigning officers to pursue established graduate courses has not been altogether satisfactory and leads us to believe that our program should be especially arranged. The experience of Harvard with its "trade unions" and Niemann fellows may allow solutions to many of our problems. Too often the ordinary graduate courses include material outside the foreign service officer's frame of reference; on the other hand, vocational courses prove rather barren in the long run, unless we specifically select certain men to acquire particular skills. The opportunities, by the Niemann program and by the various combinations, "straddles," and area groupings now in vogue, seem more to our last.

In addition to these studies there will be others of a more narrowly vocational kind. For example, one of the most important duties of the foreign service is the promotion of American trade. The Department of Commerce maintains the closest interest in this activity and we are committed to assign a good number of our officers to training under its direction. Probably most of the officers, other than probationers, who will be in training in the first years of our program will follow studies having to do with foreign trade.

There is also a keen need in our service for men with some special knowledge of modern public administration techniques. Some of our trainees will follow courses in this specialty.

So much for the outline of the training program on which

we have embarked. It is far more ambitious than anything we have attempted before and it holds more hope than anything else for the great transformation needed in our service. Compared to it, our new legislative achievements and most of our personnel arrangements are mere surface manifestations. The ground swell of real foreign service reform will start in the minds of those better men we expect to recruit and train in the future. Obviously all reforms will come to nought unless our officers have the necessary intellectual stature and creative spirit. The best legislation, the best administration, and the best will in the world cannot take the place of brains.

At worst the diplomatic mentality can be a sterile thing given to airy dilettantism, or at best it can be both creative and conservative of human values. The diplomat who has shared the lives of many peoples and has learned many disciplines is in a way a survival of humanist culture.

The winning of the war imposed on our lives and conduct a utilitarianism and a pragmatic approach which contrast in some ways with the ends for which it was fought. The wise diplomat can give meaning and direction to an engineer's and specialist's world. If our new foreign service can unite sympathy, idealism, and a world view with technical competence and modern skill it should remain as good as any in the world.

9

EDUCATION AND FOREIGN AFFAIRS:
A CHALLENGE FOR THE UNIVERSITIES

BY FREDERICK S. DUNN

THE fields of education and of public affairs share these things in common, that they are basically important to the adjustment of man to his world, and that they readily inspire misty thinking and melodious platitudes. When the two fields are united in a single discourse, there is an obvious risk of leaving behind an impressive trail of ponderous trivialities. Once it did not matter very much what was said or done about education in international relations in this country. Our position in the world was so secure that we could—and did—survive a notable degree of groping and incompetence in the conduct of American diplomacy. But we are now becoming dimly aware that our daily lives, our expectations and our hopes, our chances for orderly living in a normal world, our very survival on this planet are resting in painful measure in the hands of those who direct our foreign affairs. With two world wars just behind us and a third already casting its shadow before it, we can no longer sidestep the need for hard thinking about how to improve the chances that our relations with the rest of the world will be wisely and skillfully handled.

For alert minds, the conjunction of events of commanding importance which we face at this particular moment of history is starkly arresting. The shape which world affairs have taken is at once fraught with great danger and abundant in opportunities for creative action. From the standpoint of regularity and stability in political and social relations, the existing two-power pattern of world politics could hardly be worse. It has brought us little so far except an exhausting series of irritating crises. Yet to imaginative observers, it is far too early to assume that we have already started on a relentless march toward doom. On the contrary, it is still possible to see various ways of moving toward a more balanced world in which the risks of the present distribution of power are reduced to manageable proportions and the potentialities for improvement in social conditions are more widely realized.

In this supremely challenging situation, how can the educational institutions of the country play their full role in aiding the forces working toward reconstruction and retarding those of conflict and deterioration? What can the universities really do to improve the chances that our foreign affairs will be managed with the necessary knowledge, skill, and foresight? The answers one hears to these questions run all the way from everything to nothing. Sensible people will pay little attention to either extreme but will look in the more moderate ranges for useful answers. Here there are three obvious lines of action. The first is to increase the supply of competent men whose education fits them to be policy-makers or advisers to policy-makers. The second is to maintain, by adequate research programs, a constant stream of new knowledge, new insights, and new ideas to aid the work of decision-makers and increase our general understanding of the world in which we live. The third is to improve the education of citizens in the fundamentals of international relations so that they will have some chance of coming to terms with this most essential part of their environment and can offer the necessary support for intelligent policy decisions.

The first of these lines of action seems obvious to the point of triteness. If a greater supply of qualified policy-makers is needed, why should not the universities increase their efforts to provide them. Yet a sharp controversy has raged over the role that they can play in training future career men. On the

one hand, some institutions have frankly designed their offer-
ings in international relations simply to enable students to
qualify for particular jobs in the government service. On the
other hand, there has been strong opposition to any form of
vocationalism in the field, and this attitude has been shared
by some of the officials responsible for fixing the requirements
of the government services. The opposition sometimes goes
so far as to insist that the only proper training for prospective
policy-makers is in those courses which are most remote in time
and subject matter from the kinds of questions which they
will later have to meet.

Let us first come to terms with this question of vocational
training. What should be the aim of education in this field?
Clearly it is not that of job training for specific routinized
tasks in the government service. Certainly few universities
claim that drilling in the common procedures and skills of
diplomacy is a good substitute for a liberal education. To
assume that training in the everyday activities involved in the
management of foreign affairs is the proper way to get wise
officials is to display an egregious ignorance of what policy-
makers do, as well as of what higher education can do, to help
develop good ones.

The notion that the difference between a good diplomat and
a poor one is the possession of information about routine diplomatic procedures is surely a naïve one. It is akin to the common idea that the purpose of higher education is to stock
the mind with miscellaneous bits of information so that the
recipient merely has to fish around in his memory to pull out
the right answer to any question.

The basic difficulty with this view is, of course, that the
questions which officials beyond the clerical level have to deal
with are invariably novel in greater or less degree, and cannot
be disposed of simply by reference to information about past
events. There is no single right answer which can be dredged
up out of the memory or looked up in a book. There are al-

Frederick S. Dunn

ways alternative courses of action available, each one of which has something to be said in its favor. The act of disposing of a question is an act not merely of memory but of choosing between these alternatives. Vocational skills and information about how to handle repetitive situations are of little help in making these choices.

It may be conceded at once that no great educational paraphernalia is needed to teach the repetitive handling of known situations, and that vocational training of this kind is hardly a proper role for institutions of higher learning. For the most part, routine skills can best be taught in the service and under the supervision of actual operators.

But it is quite necessary to remember that the opposite of an erroneous proposition is not itself necessarily true. It may in fact be equally erroneous on the other side. If it is correct to say that job training as such is not the proper function of the university, it does not follow that the best training of future decision-makers is found in subjects that have no discernible relation to the types of problems which they may later face. Surely there can be no special virtue in irrelevance of subject matter as such.

For many years it has been customary to cite the example of British diplomats of the eighteenth and nineteenth centuries to support the position that a purely classical education is the best preparation for a career in international affairs. It is argued that the successes enjoyed by Great Britain in attaining its influential position in international politics must have been due in large part to the classical studies to which the members of the governing class of Britain were commonly subjected. But there is no available proof that it was the nonrelevance of the subject matter of their education to the subject matter of their careers that made British diplomacy successful. It might have been even more successful if they had also had some training in thinking in the context of the international politics of their time. In any case there is much more reason to attribute British successes in diplomacy to quite other things than the content of higher education which was traditionally pursued by prospective diplomats in those days, for example, to the special combination of circumstances which made Britain's relative power position unusually strong. One does not hear it charged today that the recent setbacks in the British position as a great power might have been due to the introduction of subject matter relevant to our times into the education of British diplomats. On the contrary, there is a growing demand in Britain that far greater attention be given to the social sciences in preparation for the civil service.

Those who argue against the inclusion of international and area studies in the training of individuals seeking careers in the field do not deny that the subject matter of international relations has become vastly more complex in recent times or that a large proportion of the questions arising in the field can be handled only by people with special knowledge. They admit that there is a definite need in particular cases for people with special training in international economics or international law and perhaps even in the institutions and cultures of particular regions. But they argue that the general run of policy questions do not call for any special knowledge or skills but rather for wisdom and common sense of a high order. From this they conclude that those who intend to be general managers of foreign affairs need no special training in international relations but only the traditional liberal arts education.

Before it is possible to arrive at a useful conclusion on the subject, it is necessary to ask in a very elementary way what kinds of intellectual activities are involved in the general conduct of international affairs.

It must be obvious that all foreign affairs, all questions of war and peace and power and welfare on the international plane, can be reduced to the making of concrete decisions by identifiable human beings. At every stage in the unfolding of any series of international events, it is possible to point to one or more persons who make choices of action and whose decisions have a direct influence on the course which events take. It is the sum of these choices which makes up the body of international relations, so far as these relations are subject to human control.

It has been known since the time of Socrates that state action was the action of individual men. In the international field, however, this truth has been obscured by the established habit of talking as if the only participants in foreign affairs were nations and not individuals. Statesmen are prone to pretend that they really have very little to do with what goes on, that it is their respective states which make the decisions and all they do is to try to carry out state policy as best they can. Scholars build whole political philosophies on the idea of states acting as independent entities with wills of their own, apart from the wills of human beings; and some legal scientists construct their juridical systems on the notion that institutions and rules of law applicable to nations can be adequate substitutes for the decision-making activities of men.

It is not to be denied that this majestic bit of ancient fiction serves many useful purposes in the regulation of human affairs. Acceptance of the decisions of government is easier if one sees them as judgments of an abstract entity rather than the always uncertain choices of human beings. Policy seems to have greater stability if offered as the edict of a nation rather than the compromise of a quarreling and frequently changing group of officials. Yet it must be clear on reflection that the kinds of acts involved in voluntary choice between alternatives can only be exercised by individuals and not by formal institutions such as the state. Where doubts exist or interests clash, some person or persons must make a conscious selection of a course of action. It is the sum of these choosing points which embodies the stormy history of man's political life, both on the national and international planes.

For some not very obvious reason, this process of choice

has not received the serious attention of those who make a practice of studying international affairs. One will look almost in vain in the books in the field for any extended consideration of the subject. Even those who go through the daily struggle of decision-making seldom write directly and candidly about it themselves, but are only concerned to convince us that the results of their thinking are not nearly as bad as they may seem to us. If we could investigate the things they actually used in arriving at their choices of action, they would too often turn out to be a strangely assorted bagful of unexamined assumptions, traditional attitudes, weak logical analysis, curbstone hypotheses unsupported by anything other than anecdotal evidence, clouded value judgments, expectations of highly doubtful validity, and blind shots in the dark. An orderly and skillful use of the tools of analysis and evaluation which have been developed over the years is an exceptional thing.

*If this is the case, it is clear that the primary task of educa*tion for prospective decision-makers and their advisers must be to provide them with the kinds of knowledge, methods, and intellectual skills that will enable them to face new questions in their field without dismay, and to use the rich resources of political and social analysis to arrive at intelligent ways of acting. There is no deep mystery about the major steps involved in rational decision-making, and if we review these briefly we can get a good idea of the methods and subject matter that would be helpful in developing the requisite skills.

In meeting any new question, the first step is obviously the orientation of the decision-maker with respect to background knowledge and facts of the case, including the recognition of the issues involved and the placing of them where they belong in the range of existing knowledge. The next step is the selection of the aim or aims to be sought. After that comes the marking out of possible alternative courses of action and the anticipation of the probable outcomes of each one. Finally comes the choice of the most promising alternative and the selection of the steps to be taken or the strategy to be pursued in following it through until the end is achieved or abandoned.

This is of course a greatly simplified picture of the hesitant trial-and-error process that normally takes place in disposing of a new question. Usually the process is an unconscious one and the intellectual activities involved are carried forward more or less simultaneously. Thus a decision-maker may achieve a more perfect orientation as he considers and discards possible courses of action. But the whole aim of his thinking is to make a prudent choice of action in the light of the values he is pursuing.

Assuredly there is no great difficulty in identifying the kinds of knowledge and methods that, if properly mastered, will help him to do this. In the first place, in order to orient himself properly, he must have a mature grasp of how the international society functions and of the major forces which are helping to mold modern civilization. This would include some awareness of the ways in which governments act in their contacts with each other and in their efforts to realize their respective interests. He should have sufficient knowledge of the influences that affect other men's behavior in political situations so that he is not constantly surprised and nonplused when they fail to conform to the patterns of his own culture.

It is equally important that he should know what is not so. He should know how to evaluate statements of alleged fact and forecasts of impending events. His background knowledge should be sufficiently extensive to prevent him from being taken in by the special pleaders for particular interests or the purveyors of bias, prejudice, and false doctrines. He should have at least enough acquaintance with modern political, economic, and social theory to know when and how much it can help him to make prudent decisions. The idea that "practical" men can eschew theory in dealing with concrete problems is, as Keynes once pointed out, quite erroneous. When they think they are doing so they are very likely merely following some old theory that has been tested and found wanting by the experts.

Against this background of information about the world in which he works and about the particular problems with which he is dealing, the decision-maker should be able to make at least a preliminary classification of the situation before him and reveal the specific nature of the question or issue. Once this is done, he has then to clarify the goal or goals to be aimed at in marking out a course of action. For effective action is not possible unless he knows in very concrete terms what he is trying to do.

Being clear about aims means being clear about values. Decision-makers in this field, no matter how skillful they may be in other ways, have an especial need for being clear about values or else they can do a great deal of damage. For the responsible decision-makers of great states have great power at their disposal. They are often in a position of being able to use military force or threat of force to back up their decisions in specific cases. In proportion to the extent of that power is their obligation to use it for enlightened aims.

The picture of diplomacy as an incessant struggle between good statesmen seeking the highest values and evil men serving their own selfish purposes is seldom a true one. Most of the time the decision-makers on *both* sides of a conflict are striving for what they regard as true values. Those who would successfully implement fundamental values in practice must possess a very practical knowledge of available methods and a ready skill in estimating the probable consequences of particular acts. History is full of instances in which good men with the best intentions have brought disaster to their people through inability to spell out successfully their basic values in terms of practicable objectives.

Clarification of values in a particular field is best acquired through practice in the application of general values to the typical concrete issues of that field. The naïve transfer of value judgments from one field to another by simple analogy, as for example from the relations between individuals to the relations between nations, often leads to confusion and sometimes to disaster.

It is not presently possible, nor is it necessary for harmonious relations, that the whole world should be subjected to one universally prescribed culture. Variety in value systems is, so far as we can now see, inescapable. The duty of national agents is not to ignore or suppress these differences but to find ways of making it possible for them to exist harmoniously side by side.

Hence policy-makers should also have a good knowledge of the value systems of other countries. If they maintain a provincial attitude and fail to understand the viewpoints of other nations, they cannot make workable decisions. But this does not mean that the decision-maker should become so saturated with the value systems of other countries that he loses sight of his own. To do so not only reduces his value as an agent of his own country, but even more as a representative in dealings with other countries. For the thing which makes him really useful to other governments is his capacity to interpret correctly and apply in concrete problems the most characteristic and firmly established values of his own people. Only in this manner is it possible to understand the basis of differences between them and to find some way of resolving those differences.

Concurrently with the development of concrete objectives goes the marking out of the alternative courses of action available. They are in fact inseparable parts of the same operation. For it is idle to spell out values in terms of objectives unless there are practical means available to reach those objectives. Similarly it is not possible to mark out available procedures unless one knows where one is proceeding.

This calls for a good deal more of the same kind of background knowledge with which the decision-maker first oriented himself in respect to the problem at hand. In addition, it calls for a knowledge of trends of events. The world the decision-maker operates in is not a stationary thing but is a constantly changing pattern of old and new happenings. Unless he is familiar not only with present facts but also with the direction in which they are developing, his knowledge of the world will not be of much use to him.

Perhaps the most important single ingredient in marking out programs for future action is the capacity to anticipate the consequences of particular acts. In the past this has been left largely to intuitive guesswork. Where the guesses were wrong (as they too frequently were), it was easy enough for the decision-maker to escape blame by pointing to the uncertainty of future events. But with our present knowledge it is often possible to obtain a fairly reliable basis for estimating the probable outcome of particular moves. Where this is so, there is no excuse for acting on the basis of blind guesswork.

Hence to his general information about the world in which he operates and the direction of significant trends, the competent decision-maker must add a command of various tools of analysis and bodies of theoretical knowledge that will aid in the making of enlightened choices of action. The analytical skills he will need consist essentially of rational devices for separating out the significant elements of a complicated situation, drawing the necessary distinctions between elements which seem superficially alike, seeing the necessary relations between apparently unconnected things, revealing the assumptions on which people are acting (including the decision-maker himself), pointing out the alternative courses of action that are available, and weighing the relative advantages of these alternatives as seen in the light of their probable outcomes.

There are men with a high native capacity for development of good judgment who can make intelligent choices of action with very little special training in a particular field. But the average man's uninformed and untrained guesswork is, in complicated social situations, not much better than random action. Without the discipline of objective analysis he is the unconscious victim of all of his private prejudices and biases, and he tends either to anticipate what he wants to happen or else to expect disaster. The result is that the expectations on which he makes his intuitive choices are wrong a far greater percentage of the time than they need to be.

There are five primary fields of general knowledge regarding human behavior in social relationships. These are politics, economics, law, history, and the group of the socio-cultural disciplines which includes sociology, anthropology, social psychology, and ethics. Each one of these fields has its counterpart in the international community: thus we have international politics, international economics, international law, diplomatic history, and the international aspects of the socio-cultural disciplines. It is to be noted, however, that these international counterparts are not merely extensions of our existing knowledge of local society to cover human relationships beyond national boundaries but are bodies of knowledge about individual and group behavior in a fundamentally different environment.

Thus international politics is not merely domestic politics applied beyond national borders but has an essential character of its own. It is true that political power operates in many ways common to all social environments, but the conduct of political relationships is different in a community in which power is centralized in a single point at the top and one in which it is not. The security of the individual unit becomes a profoundly different problem and the possibility of the resort to force is always in the background.

In a world of independent states with widely different power potentials and different value systems, there are bound to be constant rivalries and conflicts of interest. It is the business of those who are in charge of foreign affairs to manage these rivalries in such a way that they will not lead to an open struggle by force of arms. A knowledge of international politics provides the essential basis for this task. It includes not only an understanding of power relationships but also a grasp of the essential methods of mutual accommodation, conciliation, compromise, and balance. Only where the conditions of effective action are known and understood by those responsible for the conduct of international affairs is it possible to carry on an extensive and mutually advantageous community life on the international plane without the constant danger of war.

In like manner, international trade is not merely an extension beyond national borders of domestic trade, but is in some ways a different subject calling for its own skills and bodies of knowledge. Trade across national borders is trade complicated by the actions of different national governments, each one seeking to protect or improve the position of its own nationals. That situation is quite different from the one in which transactions are completed within the range of a single governmental authority presumably acting for the benefit of the whole community. In the case of international trade, it would be much easier if we could assume that the actions of each government were taken on behalf of the world community as a whole but, under the present organization of international society, it is not even supposed that national governments will act in such a manner. Their officials are expected to be much more concerned about the welfare of the citizens of their own nation than about the citizens of other nations, and to formulate their politics accordingly.

It is true that, within these basic conditions, it is possible to carry on an extensive and profitable trade across national boundaries. But this is possible only if those in charge of state actions understand these complicated conditions and know how to operate effectively within them.

Similarly, it would be a mistake to assume that international law is merely an extension of domestic law beyond national boundaries. While a habit of observing rules of law might have the same effect on human conduct in both spheres, the conditions under which laws are made and applied are fundamentally different. The absence of a central enforcement agency may not prevent laws from influencing conduct on a wide scale, but it does have an unquestioned effect upon the kinds of rules which will be accepted by independent nations and applied effectively by them. International lawyers who ignore the essential difference between the national and international communities are merely giving in to false hopes. The effective leaders in this field who have succeeded in extending the control of international conduct by rules of law, from Grotius to the present time, have invariably been those who took full account of the conditions under which a system of law could operate in the international field, and knew how to make the most effective use of those conditions.

The value of the historical method for future practitioners lies primarily in the fact that it makes possible learning from past experience. The history of international relations, or diplomatic history as it is commonly called, if properly organized, can afford considerable guidance to statesmen in making choices between alternative courses of action in international problems. It is difficult to see how any man can make wise decisions without a wide knowledge of history. Yet unfortunately a large part of what has been labeled diplomatic history has been of little or no value in improving the quality of the expectations on which decision-makers could act intelligently. Much of it has been written by historians who had very little understanding of the theory of international politics. There is a mass of source material available for this purpose but only in recent years have the writers of the history of diplomacy begun to make good use of it. Prior to that time diplomatic history tended to be both nationally biased and unanalytical.

Finally, the work of anthropologists, sociologists, and social psychologists often has great value for practitioners in the international field, but it generally needs evaluation and application by those who are familiar with the field itself. The uncritical transfer of generalizations drawn from the data of local groups to the relationships of highly complex states is apt to be misleading. But, with this reservation, it is true that those who make decisions on foreign policy can be saved many mistakes and much bewilderment if they have a competent understanding of some of the findings of the creative scholars in these subjects.

Within these five basic fields of knowledge is found most of what we know about individual and group behavior in international relationships and about the environment which conditions such behavior. Not all of these fields have been equally well cultivated by scholars in the past, but great progress has been made in recent years in building up a body of basic knowledge about international relations, and the lack of such knowledge is no longer a serious obstacle to the development of an adequate program of education for future decision-makers and their advisers.

There accordingly appears to be no great difficulty in marking out what the role of the universities should be in the effort to increase the supply of competent decision-makers in international affairs.[1] On the undergraduate level, there exists a rich and varied field of knowledge through which it is possible to begin the development of the aptitudes and skills needed in the intelligent handling of foreign affairs. The basic elements of international relations can be fitted into a program of general education without sacrificing the values normally derived from a liberal arts course. The training in the uses of the mind, the organization of capacities in a serviceable way to deal with significant social problems, the clarification of value preferences, and the acquisition of a systematic body of in-

---

[1] On this general subject see the admirable book by Grayson L. Kirk on *The Study of International Relations,* published in 1947 by the Council on Foreign Relations, New York.

formation about the modern world can be carried on to a large extent within the context of the field itself.

The field has another advantage from the standpoint of general education. Since it deals with whole problems rather than with fractions of them and calls for familiarity with several disciplines, it avoids the danger of early overspecialization and tends to diminish the importance of existing boundaries between subjects.

The main problem in making out a program of studies in the undergraduate curriculum is, of course, that of time. The amount of concentration that is normally allowed in a major field is not large and the most that can be hoped for is a generous introduction to the main branches of the subject. At the present time some universities offer courses in international politics (including political geography), international economics, international law and organization, diplomatic history and various area studies. Within this framework it is possible to make a good start on the accumulation of the necessary basic information and to acquire a familiarity with the methods of thinking that have proved fruitful in the past.

It must be clear, however, that, considering the immense complexity and scope of the field, the amount that can be accomplished in the undergraduate years is not much more than a beginning. It is not generally possible within this time to turn out technicians, i.e. those who have some competence in applying the existing body of general knowledge to specific questions. For this some additional work on the graduate level would seem to be required.

In graduate work the purposes which animate students are almost always professional in character. But again this does not or should not mean training in the routine procedures of specific jobs, but in the capacities required to arrive at intelligent decisions in new and complex issues. This means not only the accumulation of more knowledge but the greater mastery of analytical skills. The problem-solving type of instruction which is common in graduate work is particularly well adapted to these aims.

There is some difference, of course, in the professional training that would be required by those who intend to be practitioners or technicians, i.e. those whose primary business is to apply knowledge to practical situations, and scholars or research workers whose aim is to increase the sum of general knowledge in the field. The skills required by the practitioner can often be developed in actual practice, assuming, of course, that he has the proper start. The scholar, on the other hand, must normally acquire his training through academic studies, although this naturally does not exclude practical experience. Hence, it is often held that some difference is justified in the length and scope of the graduate programs offered to prospective practitioners and prospective scholars. But it is important to remember that both of them require intellectual talents of the highest order, and if the practitioner can get on with less graduate work, it is because suitable provision has been made for the maturation of his capacities in the practice of his profession.

Present arguments against graduate work for those seeking general careers in international relations are two: (1) many good decision-makers have got on without it; (2) those who have graduate degrees will not want to spend much time on routine tasks.

The first argument is similar to the claim that the atomic bomb is not very important because a massed bomber attack with regular bombs can destroy a city almost as effectively as an atom bomb. But the obvious answer is that if the planes carrying the usual type of bombs were equipped instead with atom bombs, their destructive power would be enormously increased. So it is with the man who has natural talents for efficient decision-making. He may be good without much training, but he would doubtless be a lot better if his capacities were well organized and developed in the beginning by appropriate professional training.

In regard to the objection that people with some professional training will be dissatisfied with small tasks, the proper course would seem to be, not to retard the training of those who are qualified for more complicated assignments, but to reclassify the routine activities in such a way that more of them can be handled by clerical personnel. If it turned out that eventually there were too many well-trained men for the number of positions available, one can assume that the normal workings of supply and demand would sooner or later bring about an adjustment.

In any case the problem is not merely that of providing a single type of training for a single kind of all-around official, but rather of developing a diversity of talents and skills for a number of different tasks. The universities have to be prepared to offer a varied program of graduate training to meet the needs of both generalists and specialists. A beginning has been made in a few places toward providing an adequate program, but in general there is still some confusion as to the aims which should be sought in higher education in this field. Such confusion can be avoided by a careful appraisal of the kinds of intellectual activities which are involved in the intelligent conduct of foreign affairs and the resources which the social sciences have to offer in organizing and developing the relevant capacities.

The second line of action that the universities can follow in helping to get better decision-making is to increase the facilities for research in the field. The objectives of this work are both to aid in the analysis and understanding of the complex problems of foreign affairs and to add to the sum of existing knowledge about how nations behave in their relations with each other.

There can hardly be any rational question about the desirability of giving this work every possible encouragement. The problems of international relations today are so complex and so threatening that it is immensely important to have all possible help in comprehending them and in working toward solutions. To the extent that the universities can aid in throwing light on these problems, it would seem to be a duty of high priority.

To such problems the scholar can bring not only his knowledge and analytical skills but also some degree of detachment. Generally he is not personally involved in advancing any particular solution and hence can consider all the possibilities. There is a natural tendency for those who are constantly making decisions under pressure to become attached to their first offhand answers and to spend more time in fortifying their beliefs than in looking for the holes in them. Scholars, on the other hand, need take on only those questions for which there are time and suitable methods for analysis.[2] They can afford the luxury of suspended judgment until the essential material is in. They have the opportunity for reflection which sometimes gives them insights not apparent to those immediately involved in action.

In any case, the number of complex international questions now facing the nation is huge and the number of people equipped to handle them is woefully small. There is every reason for the universities to expand their facilities for research in this field to the greatest possible extent that is commensurate with the maintenance of the necessary standards.

Two reasons have been advanced why scholars should not devote their time to international problems of current importance. One is that they do not generally have access to secret documents. The other is that they should concern them-

[2] See on this point the inaugural lecture by Professor E. L. Woodward before the University of Oxford, February 17, 1945, on "The Study of International Relations at a University," Oxford University Press, 1945.

selves with the more permanent aspects of knowledge and should avoid the transient and the unique issues.

The hampering effect of lack of access to confidential files has been greatly exaggerated. Most of the time the issues involved in important situations are easy enough to define, even though the latest documents are not available. Frequently an expert diagnostician can guess the general tenor of exchanges of correspondence without actually seeing them. In any case, there are plenty of vital issues troubling the decision-makers in which all the material that is really important is available. It is the common testimony of experienced political analysts that, while access to secret documents would frequently make their work much easier, the lack of it is seldom a real obstacle to fertile analysis of current problems.

The notion that scholars should not concern themselves with practical problems of the present but only with the accumulated knowledge of the past seems to be based on a strange idea of how the great political analysts of the past themselves spent their time. In fact they were deeply concerned with the concrete political and social problems of their own day. In the ages when this has not been so, the writings of political theorists have tended to be barren of fresh ideas, and to sink into a quagmire of purely doctrinal disputes.

No real scholar questions the importance of going to the past wherever possible to get light on the problems of the day. None denies the value of intensive study of the more permanent findings dredged up by other scholars out of human experience. Yet this is not incompatible with the focusing of attention on basic policy issues of the modern world.

The question is not in fact of an either/or type. It is not necessary to choose between exclusive concern with ephemeral current events or an ivory-tower isolation from the modern world. One of the best ways of getting at truths of enduring value is through the intensive study of the hard realities of present day issues. The constant diagnosis of important current conflicts is an excellent corrective for the pedant's tendency to get lost in the endless verbal tunnels of abstract doctrinal speculation.

It is necessary, of course, to use some discretion in choosing the issues to be studied. Some questions which receive great popular attention are not suitable for the study of research scholars because no effective methods of analysis have been developed for them or because they offer no prospect of yielding anything of permanent value. But there are many questions to which the scholar can bring some light by his knowledge and methods of analysis, and which at the same time offer an opportunity to add something of enduring value to existing knowledge.

The types of training so far considered have been for those who intend to be careerists in the field, whether as practitioners or as scholars. There is another training function for the universities which is equally pressing and that is the education of citizens in the intelligent understanding of important international problems and policies.

Again the need for this activity seems so obvious that it is hardly necessary to state it. How is it possible for democratic government to operate in the present tightly woven world unless there is full opportunity for citizens to be well informed on the great issues on which their government must have a policy? How is it possible for the citizen to find a satisfactory adjustment to his world unless he has some means of understanding and reacting to the important political and social forces that bear down upon him? Yet until very recent times, there has been little recognition of the need for preparing the layman for effective thinking about foreign affairs. There has even been some doubt about the academic respectability of public education in the field.

One reason for this may have been the fact that such education as was attempted was often wretchedly done and the materials used were undeniably bad. Not much can in fact be said for the traditional international events course which ignored the realities of international politics and misled the student with vastly oversimplified pictures of current issues. Most of the time these courses were given by teachers who themselves had had no specialized training in international relations.

But because an essential function was indifferently performed in the past is no reason for concluding that it should not be undertaken at all. On the contrary it is an argument for giving greater attention to the subject in order that the right methods and standards may be developed.

There is at last being opened up a supply of teachers who are capable of teaching international relations in a competent way as part of the general education of laymen. There are also being developed some materials on the subject which teachers can offer their students without apology. The time is approaching when there will no longer be much excuse for offering shoddy courses in current events under the guise of instruction in international relations.

It has already been argued above that on the undergraduate level the subject of international relations should be taught as part of general education and not as a vocational subject. This is of course especially true for those who have no intention of finding careers in the field. Happily the subject is one which, if properly organized, has high educational value both in teaching the ways of effective thought and in introducing the student to some important bodies of literature. It provides an admirable medium for enabling the student to acquire some familiarity with political analysis and with the kinds of issues he will later have to face constantly in his efforts to come to terms with his environment.

Today's greatest danger is perhaps the overwhelming pressure for a resolution of the current two-power conflict by some dramatic action, such as a Soviet-American war. Only if advances are made on the three levels of understanding of research, university instruction, and adult education will this danger be eliminated. For then a responsible decision-maker backed up by an enlightened and patient public opinion can make an unspectacular series of small (but correct) decisions instead of a single dramatic (but possibly categorically wrong) big decision.

PART IV
THE BRITISH EXPERIENCE

10

THE BRITISH CIVIL SERVICE

BY SIR JAMES GRIGG

IN this essay, I am, I imagine, expected to tell something of the position the English (and of course the Scottish, the Welsh, and some of the Irish) universities occupy in relation to the British public service. I think that this can best be brought out in the course of a description of the methods by which the upper reaches of our civil service are recruited. The methods have varied from time to time but they have followed a fairly coherent and logical course of development except for two serious breaks occasioned by the special circumstances of the two world wars and their aftermaths. What I would propose to do then is first to describe in the broadest outline this developing process from the time I entered the service, with such commentary—relevant or irrelevant—as may occur to me at different stages, and then to give an account of the emergency system of recruitment which is now in force for the immediate postwar years. Since Professor Woodward is writing about the foreign service, nothing that I am going to say will apply to that.

Let me, by way of preliminary, pick out what seem to me three dominant and persisting factors governing our civil service. The first is the very sharp line of division between the politician and the civil servant. The second is the permanent character of the service, and the third is that it is, and has been for most of a hundred years, recruited by open competition.

First—the relation of the civil servant to the politician. In our country, the political heads of departments sit in one or other of the two Houses of Parliament—nearly all of them in

147

the Commons. They are jointly responsible for the political program and actions of the government and individually (subject to the overriding collective Cabinet responsibility) answerable for the policy and conduct of their departments. Insofar as the policy involves new legislation they have personally to conduct it through the legislature. In addition, they have to persuade Parliament to vote the funds for carrying on the work of the department and they are subject to daily interpellation and can on occasion be made the subject of specific votes of censure. In their spare time they defend and commend their policy to the electors but predominantly in their own constituencies. Thus, I take it that a British minister has to spend a far greater proportion of his time in Parliament than his opposite number in the American Congress. He has also the rather laborious task of looking after a constituency and of getting himself reelected from time to time, though in the last analysis the American minister too is a bird of passage whose time of passage depends on the caprices of the electorate and on his capacity to maintain harmony with his political colleagues.

The permanency of the civil servant is, as I mentioned above, another dominant factor governing our civil service. He enters the service with the expectation of devoting his whole working life to it. He enjoys certain pension rights which increase with his period of service and his growing remuneration as he advances in the service, but these pension rights are dependent on his serving to the age of sixty or until he is permanently incapacitated. He can, of course, leave the service before sixty but if he does all his pension rights lapse. Moreover, he is under a moral obligation not to make his new career in a concern which has had contractual relationships with the department in which he has been working. To avoid possible misunderstandings, I had better say that in times of pressure—in war particularly—the government can and does employ large numbers of temporary civil servants but these acquire no rights against the state except that of a decent period of notice before discharge. Permanent civil servants cannot be sacked outright except for some grave misconduct or gross inefficiency but there are usually ways and means of sliding misfits in one department to more suitable work in another. They can reasonably expect steady promotion up to a certain point but beyond that they are subject to the rigorous test of selection on merit.

From the contrast between the ephemeral politician and the permanent civil servant, I note three things: First, that civil servants rarely become politicians. If they do, it is almost invariably after retirement on pension and this takes place at an age which precludes a prolonged political career. As a matter of fact, there is a definite legal ban on a man being at once a civil servant and a politician.

Then again, ministers are so much occupied with Parliament and politics that they have perforce to leave the actual administration of their departments very largely in the charge of their civil servants, particularly, of course, the senior ones. And lastly, civil servants have no public identity. All their deeds or misdeeds fall on the minister, to be defended or explained by him as if they were his own acts. They do not talk to the press or appear before Parliament and there is a reasonably well-observed convention that they are not attacked by name or particular designation either in Parliament or in the press.

I now come to the third characteristic—viz. recruitment by open competition. This, in normal conditions, is the rule over a very large part of the civil service. It does not invariably apply to what are known as the minor and manipulative grades or to workmen in such departments as the post office and the admiralty dockyards. It does apply by and large to stenographers, to the various professional grades such as architects, engineers, and lawyers employed on purely legal work. It applies to special grades such as inspectors of taxes or to Ministry of Labor officers. And above all, it applies to the three basic classes which are, generally speaking, common to all the major departments—viz. the clerical, the executive, and the administrative.

These three basic classes go to make up the distinctive structure of the civil service. The open examinations for all three are subject to age limits which are fixed with regard to three fairly well-defined stages in our educational system. Clericals are recruited at 16 or 17 and this range of age corresponds to the conclusion of three years spent in a secondary school after a much longer time spent in a primary or elementary school. The executive class come in at 18 or 19 at what would normally be the conclusion of a secondary school career, for those who do not aspire to go on to a degree course at the university. The administrative class age is 21 to 24 which allows for the completion of a full honors degree course at a university.

The duties of the clericals are exactly what the name implies: executives are charged, in effect, with the execution or carrying out of government policy or legislation along fairly clearly marked lines; the administrative class is intended to provide the general managerial capacity. They work out detailed policy and legislation in accordance with the political directions of ministers: they are responsible for the management of their departments, again under the general orders of ministers, and they are supposed to be adaptable enough to be able to take—with the minimum of time—the higher permanent places in any of the departments, even though they may never have previously served in them.

Promotion from clerical to executive or from executive to administrative is always possible where special merit is shown and takes place freely, though not so freely as to damage the prospects or rather the career value of those who enter the higher class through the prescribed examination channel.

What the universities are concerned with is, in the main, the administrative class and from now on, in speaking of the civil service, I shall be referring only to that class unless the context makes clear otherwise.

I entered the service in 1913 and it must be remembered that at that time people still believed one could have too much government. The examination was a combined one for the Home, Indian, and Colonial Services and, of some sixty or seventy vacancies, not more than ten or a dozen would relate to the Home service. There was only one compulsory subject—English essay—and there was no interview mark. Candidates were allowed to offer subjects up to a very high maximum and the subjects were more or less coextensive with those of the prevailing final honor schools at the universities. The syllabus therefore excluded the more esoteric subjects in which it is now possible to get a degree and it did not give great weight to law or economics. Perhaps you would bear with me if I give the subjects which I myself took. The highest mark permissible was 6000. My list and the allotted maxima were as follows:

English Essay	500	One three-hour paper
Mathematics	2400	8 papers
Chemistry⎫		
Physics ⎬ 600 each	1800	2 papers plus a practical test
Botany ⎭		for each of the three
English Literature	600	2 papers—one relating to a set period
Economics	600	2 papers

From this example it will be pretty clear that to have a good chance of getting one of the Home vacancies the candidate must have reached a good class in one of the final honor schools but that this alone was not enough. It was necessary to offer other subjects and to reach a reasonably high standard in them too. In other words he had to know a great deal about one group of subjects and quite a lot about some other subjects. It must be remembered that the object of this examination was

James Grigg

to produce persons of general managerial capacity—people who may not know all about everything but who are capable of learning almost anything and who know where to find people who do know about the things they don't. It discouraged therefore the pure specialist and it discouraged the smatterer. So much was the last true that the examiners used to deduct from the marks a man got in any paper a quarter of the marks he didn't get. For example if his gross mark was 80 per cent he could actually count 75 per cent but if it was 40 per cent he could only score 25 per cent. When the results of the examination were available candidates were allowed to choose, in order, to which service (Home, Indian, or Colonial) they wished to be appointed and, if they chose the Home service, which of the declared vacancies they preferred. In practice the Home vacancies were all filled from candidates towards the top of the list and among those who chose the Home service, the first few candidates elected the treasury. There were a number of reasons for this choice of the treasury. First the scales of pay were somewhat better than in most other departments. Secondly the range of work was wider in the treasury and the responsibility and authority greater than elsewhere. Apart from all the high-flying or pure—if that is a suitable word to use— finance, the treasury was charged with the whole business of expenditure control, both general and particular. Moreover it was responsible for fixing establishments and the conditions of service of all government servants. And in addition it had certain coordinating functions in the matter of the methods and machinery of government business. From this it followed that the treasury-trained official had a better chance of promotion either in his own or to some other department.

I hope that it will have become obvious—if it hasn't, I have sadly failed in perspicuity—that in my young days our administrative class examination system tended to favor those who had a broad education in the more humane subjects, combined with real proficiency in one group of them. I admit that my own particular combination of mathematics and natural science had in theory the same chance as the more cultured groups but even so I found it necessary to offer English literature and economics in addition. And anyhow it was certainly true in those days that quite an indecent proportion of the people who got to the top of the treasury were men whose first subject was classics with another of the humanities as a second line. If I had the chance to go back to 1912 and 1913 again I would certainly select mathematics and history as my two groups but then I regard this particular mixture as very nearly the ideal education in general as well as providing the best preliminary training for the public service. Be all this as it may, the pre-World War I system did not cater to the technician; it ruled out the pure specialist; and it certainly discouraged the smatterer. It would also be true to say that the great bulk of those who entered the administrative class came from Oxford or Cambridge.

I have perhaps spent an undue time on the system which prevailed more than thirty years ago but I think it will be found as I go on that quite a number of its essential features have endured or at any rate endured until the outbreak of World War II.

I now come to World War I. Naturally the examination entry was suspended throughout the war and when peace came it was found that the sphere of government had become materially enlarged. Special measures had to be taken to fill both the accumulated shortage and the enhanced requirement and these took the form of qualifying test plus selection with a good deal of weightage for men who had served with distinction in the armed forces during the war. After a few years the examination system was restored but with some diffeiences. The scope of the compulsory part of the examination was greatly enlarged and it now included both English essay and English language, everyday science, current affairs and a very heavily marked interview or *viva voce* test. This compulsory section covered about 40 per cent of the total possible marking. The remaining 60 per cent covered the general university curricula as before, only with a certain number of fancy subjects added, but with no extra weightage for law and economics. I suppose that the general effect of these changes was somewhat to diminish the necessity of a very good degree standard in one group of subjects and to enhance the requirement of what for a better phrase I shall call "man of the world"-liness. It was, if anything, even more calculated than before to discourage the specialist and the smatterer. I suppose too that it somewhat discounted the previous favoring of the humanities as against the more modern subjects but it was very far from encouraging candidates to take the law or economics schools.

At about the same time the treasury differential in pay disappeared while the treasury became, if possible, even more important by the recognition of its permanent secretary as the head of the civil service and the adviser of the Prime Minister on general service matters especially those concerning the higher appointments. Very soon, too, it ceased to take candidates direct from the examination and it recruited its staff at all the administrative levels from the best individuals in the other departments.

Personally, I always felt some doubt about most of these so-called improvements and I thought that I could discern some falling off in standards generally and in those of the treasury in particular. On the other hand I am bound to say that the habit of thinking that "things aren't what they were in my young days" develops at a revoltingly early period of middle life and, what is perhaps more to the point, that any system which is required to produce fifty or sixty men a year is at a considerable disadvantage as against one which is called upon for no more than a dozen.

In the early inter-war years, women too became eligible to compete for administrative appointments but I refrain from drawing any moral from this fact.

British Civil Service

By and large the system established in the early 'twenties lasted till just before World War II. In about 1937, the lower age limit was reduced from 22 to 21. Everyday science was taken out of the compulsory list, and the optional list maximum was reduced to little more than half of the total. At the same time, the optional list was extended to cover even more esoteric subjects while the weightage for law and economics was materially increased.

For my part I regard nearly all these changes as retrograde. It certainly increased the encouragement to specialize, it tended to diminish the encouragement to a humanitarian education, and it attracted more and more of the students who gave their main attention to law and economics. On the other hand, I thoroughly approve the added inducement given to proficiency in the English language. A good administrative civil servant must not only be able to set out clearly and with absence of rigmarole what it is he wants to do, but he must be able to explain to his political masters in the same way why he wants to do it. That is one of the reasons why I think that the practice at Oxford and Cambridge of making undergraduates, whatever their subject, write at least one essay a week is so valuable. Having said this, I am afraid I have to confess that at Cambridge in my day, mathematicians and scientists were exempt from this salutary discipline and that it was precisely this combination of subjects which I offered. However, if I had my time over again, I would certainly not choose this particular unholy alliance. The lowering of the age was perhaps intended to give the more modern universities a greater chance but nevertheless in 1939 it was still true that 85 per cent of the successful candidates came from Oxford and Cambridge. I don't think that this is necessarily to be deplored even on an anti-snob basis for the very large majority of the entrants to the two ancient universities would hardly be there but for scholarships. Moreover, many of the best students from the newer universities make a point of going on to Oxford or Cambridge.

James Grigg

By now it will have become clear that the author of these remarks is a bit of a shellback—I am sorry I was not in the United States long enough to learn the equivalent American expression—or perhaps like tobacco and the potato it originally came from that continent. It will also be obvious that he is not a believer in the value of the law or economics faculties as a training for the general administrative part of the public service. At the risk of being thought tiresomely provocative I will give some of the reasons for my prejudices against law and economics. I think my objection to the law is that, for anything but the practice of the law, it has a narrowing influence. Lawyers should therefore be employed preponderantly in their purely professional capacity and personally I would come very near to regarding *expertise* in law as a positive disqualification for a type of administration which requires a man to be a wise manager with a wide general outlook and culture, and who is concerned much more with arriving at sensible working arrangements than at the narrow and exact legal truth. Of course his sensible working arrangements must have regard to the legal possibilities but he can easily get from the lawyers expert advice as to whether what he wants to do is likely to be challenged in the courts.

As regards economics, let me say that it pretends far too often to be an exact science. But in fact one is sometimes tempted to say of it *"quot homines tot sententiae."* Indeed it is worse than that, for I expect most of you have heard of the old jibe "wheresoever there are five economists there will be six opinions and two of them will be Keynes's!" So that altogether it offers a very imperfect guide to those who have to act and not to deliberate. Then again, I do not like the tendency which some writers seem to have of proving to their own satisfaction that qualities or habits which in private individuals have for hundreds of years been regarded as virtues add up in the mass to a collective vice or folly. And further, I think it is often forgotten that economics must be conditioned by politics, which I

156

take it is what its earlier name of political economy was intended to connote. What I have particularly in mind here is that no conclusion at which men may arrive by pure economic reasoning can ever be integrally carried into effect in a political organism unless that organism is a completely totalitarian one. In ordinary democratic conditions it is impossible to assume that the resultant of individual actions is what it ought to be if economic theory is to be carried into practice. So long as man has any freedom of action or choice he is bound to do quite often what his all-wise governors want him not to do and what he would not do if he too were infinitely wise. But liberty to be unwise as well as wise over a wide range of activity is an essential element in any tolerable system. A second aspect of this same question is the tendency of political parties to adopt as their distinctive hallmark a particular economic doctrine without regard to the limitations of time or place or circumstance which qualify its validity. I need only refer here to free trade *vs.* protection or private enterprise *vs.* state ownership. Altogether I conclude that the place of the man who is predominantly an economist is as the adviser of the administrator rather than as the actual administrator. Finally, so far as economics is concerned, may I refer to its statistical side. A passion for collecting facts—all the facts which may conceivably be relevant to a particular problem—is very liable to interfere with the capacity or power of the administrator to see the wood for the trees and arrive at a common sense workable solution of the problem quickly. I don't mean to say that he should be a pure empiricist but a good solution today or tomorrow is nearly always better than a much more perfect one next month. Needless to say, I do not want to imply that the administrator ought not to have read sufficient economics to be able to know what a professional economist is talking about. But he needn't have done an honors course at a university for this.

I have two further disjointed observations to make before I come to describe the present emergency system of recruitment for the administrative class. A few pages back I referred casually to the two special grades of inspectors of taxes and employment officers of the Ministry of Labor. These have an examination to themselves, the age limits for which are now the same as those for the administrative class. This examination tends to attract men and women from the younger universities rather than from Oxford or Cambridge presumably because the syllabus is more weighted in the direction of practical and non-humane subjects. I do not know much about the Ministry of Labor but I was for three years chairman of the Board of Inland Revenue and got to know a great deal of the work of the inspectors of taxes. I can testify that they are a very high class article. Never did a body of men extract so much money from so many people with so near an approach to general acquiescence. At first sight this seems to contradict my preference for the humanities as an education but I make two answers to any accusation of inconsistency. The inspectors of taxes are much more specialists than general managers of large concerns and moreover in their early years they have one priceless advantage in that they are thrown on their own very soon after they enter the service and I have always understood that being thrown into the water is the best way of learning to swim. This, by a somewhat unadroit mixing of metaphors, releases the, I hope, final bee from my bonnet.

I do not believe in institutes or faculties or theoretical courses of public administration. In our system, at any rate, much the most important requirement is the ability to manage men—whether they are our fellow civil servants subordinate to us or the more senior civil servants and the politicians above us or whether, again, it is the man in the street who is at once the toad under our barrow and our ultimate master. And I am convinced that the art of managing men cannot be imparted in schools or university courses or public lectures. Like most of the really important capacities, it can only be acquired by learning to do it in practice.

British Civil Service

Now let me come to the emergency system of recruitment.

As a result of the war the civil service suffered severe dilution, particularly in the higher classes. Naturally the prime cause was the expansion of the range of government activities and the fact that this expansion takes a long time to subside. Some of the wartime controls and undertakings have necessarily to be liquidated slowly while others look as if they are becoming permanent at any rate in England, where we now have a government whose policy is the more conscious direction of the economic life of the nation. There was, moreover, a complete suspension of the normal methods of recruitment during the war as it would have been quite unfair, if not impracticable, to hold open examinations when so large a proportion of the nation's manpower had been diverted to urgent war work. And finally, though normal recruitment ceased, the normal casualties due to deaths, incapacity, and retirements did not. The dilution has been particularly serious in the administrative class and it can be illustrated in a somewhat startling way by taking the figures as of 1945 of one of the main ranks in that class. Its over-all strength was 1,200, but of that 1,200, only 200 were entrants via the prewar open competition for the administrative class. About 600 were permanent civil servants who had been promoted from the lower classes and another 400 were war temporaries—most of them, I think, university graduates.

It has now been decided to restore the principle of open competition as quickly as possible. But this will not be practicable for the administrative class until 1949 by which time it will be possible for candidates to have completed a full university course since the end of the war. For lower classes, open competition can be and is being restored somewhat earlier. But meantime the need for recruits is dire and there are in addition the wants and claims of all those leaving the fighting services who, but for the war, would have been able to make their life's career in the civil service. Hence the special so-

James Grigg

called reconstruction scheme. For some of the lower classes, the reconstruction scheme will be running for a time side by side with the normal open competitive system. Theoretically it is possible for the ex-service man, with the help of a suitable age allowance for his war service, to sit for the ordinary examination but by and large his interests will be cared for by reserving for him a high proportion of the vacancies assigned to the reconstruction scheme. For the administrative class this reconstruction scheme involves the establishment in the higher grades of a comparatively small number of those older men who have rendered distinguished service in a temporary capacity during the war and who, as I said earlier, were generally speaking university graduates. But in the main the scheme embodies a special competition for all men and women of not more than thirty years of age subject to the reservation of three quarters of the vacancies for ex-service candidates. To be eligible for the competition, candidates must have had at least one year's residence at a university and either a second (or better) class honors degree or a certificate from the university authorities that they would have got such a degree if they had been able to complete their course. The competition itself consists of a simple written examination—arithmetic, English, general knowledge, plus a series of intelligence tests—together with two of what I may call personality tests. The first of these personality tests is an adaptation of the system which has in a somewhat pejorative sense come to be known as the "country-house" system. This was invented by the War Office for the selection of junior military officers during the war. Incidentally, I may remark that in our caste-ridden army all candidates for wartime commissions had to have served in the ranks. Under the country-house system a group of candidates actually live in a mess with the members of an interviewing board for three days or so and undergo the scrutiny of the lynxes during meals, recreation, and during formal interviews, individual or collective. In the War Office system the board invariably contained

160

a psychologist or a psychiatrist—I am never sure which or if there is any difference—but this feature has disappeared in the civil service system. Having been responsible for the War Office practice I can well understand this. I have no doubt that psychologists or psychiatrists—whichever it is—are very clever people but I am not sure that they were always very wise. No doubt they knew all about abnormalities but they sometimes seemed to me to be pretty obtuse in the face of outstanding normality. And some of their Freudian questions used to infuriate and disgust those highly normal beings who make up the great majority of an O.C.T.U. and this fury led in turn to outraged questions in Parliament to the Secretary of State for War. However, this is a digression and I had better come back to my muttons. The candidates who reach a certain standard in the written examination go on to one of these country-house parties. Incidentally, it has been found that some persons of very high academic distinction have failed to pass this simple qualifying test. In the light of the reports of the country-house hosts, candidates go to a final interview board of the Civil Service Commission which is in fact a selection as well as an interview board. It will be obvious from what I have said that the universities have a virtual monopoly of these immediate postwar entrants to the administrative class. And though what I said in the first part of my essay about the value of particular courses taken at the university for the purpose of getting into the service may not be valid, I think that what I said about the courses which are most likely to generate the qualities which make for success in the service is entirely applicable. In brief, these are the qualities which produce the general manager rather than the specialist: one who can manage men; who can delegate; who knows where to find everything and everybody he wants—if you like, the person who is wise rather than outstandingly clever, but who is clever enough to know what he is looking for.

And now one brief word about the staffing of the boards

which under the new government policy will run the newly nationalized industries. These will not be civil servants in the ordinary sense. The boards will very largely have control of their own recruitment and employment policies and they will certainly start largely by taking over people already in the industries. Whether they will later on look more to the universities it is too early to say. At present the government is lending or seconding to them a small number of civil servants to ease the period of transition from private to state control. And that is about all I can say about what is certain to be a very interesting and important question in the future.

Finally, I would like to cite a short passage from an article I once wrote in the Sunday *Times* about the civil service: "It is above everything incorruptible—in spite of some lowering of standards due to its wartime dilution. It is also extremely efficient in that it rarely, if ever, fails to carry out adequately the policies laid down by ministers and Parliament. It is loyal and impartial—loyal to ministers whatever the party in power, and even-minded and just to all members of the public whatever their circumstances. It is on the whole, hard-working, conscientious and public-spirited, and it is astonishingly meek in the face of the mostly undeserved public assaults on it." I am not sure that I altogether applaud the meekness, but that is by the way. What is clear is that it is a very remarkable organism and I hope I have made it plain that in its upper or management reaches it recruits very largely from the universities. And I think the English universities—and Scottish and Welsh and some of the Irish—have every reason to be proud of the contribution they are making to the governance of our country—a contribution which looks as if it were becoming greater in extent, more complex and difficult and more vital in the years which now confront us.

Up to this point I have not covered the blessed subject of coordination. What I have to say about this does not fit readily into my main remarks and so I propose to present it quite shamelessly as an afterthought. Of course, in a simple Jeffersonian world, where government minds its own business and doesn't try to do everybody else's, there ought to be no need of coordination. The very minor amount of necessary government business can be allocated to a small number of departments without overlapping. No conflict of jurisdiction can possibly arise and governments always speak with one voice. But this ideal world no longer exists and it looks as if it never will exist again. It is therefore not practicable in these days to allocate government business without overlapping and hence the need for coordination. I am tempted to turn aside here and animadvert on the economic waste of having to use so many fine brains on coordination, and on the very serious danger that coordination may be misused so as to produce utter inaction and stagnation. But perhaps I have already been sufficiently controversial.

I had the advantage recently of reading a very acute American study of the British administrative system. In it there was an examination of this very subject of coordination and in particular of two rival theories on how it is achieved. According to the first of these, coordination is brought about by the administrative class as a whole, who are pictured as a kind of religious order. They are said to dress alike, to eat together and take the opportunity provided by their syssitia to fix everything up in an efficient and agreeable way. The second theory holds that coordination is performed by the cabinet secretariat which was fashioned by the amazingly efficient Lord Hankey. There is something in both theories but in my view there is a third agency which is more important than either—namely the Treasury.

The religious order thesis has this much to be said in its favor, namely that the members of the administrative class have lots of things in common: their provenance from the universities—nearly always Oxford or Cambridge; they belong to a body which is at least as much a service as the army or navy;

they are permanent; they are quite frequently moved about from one department to another; the heads of the different departments mostly sit together on the Joint Whitley Council for the civil service as a whole; a very high proportion of the whole of them belong to one or other of not more than half a dozen clubs in the Pall Mall area. They have thus abundant chance of talking shop together and I am bound to confess from many years of experience that the chance is abundantly used and not infrequently abused.

For the cabinet secretariat thesis, it can indubitably be claimed that they do a great deal to secure that disputed matters are referred to the Cabinet for adjudication and that, either by the mechanism of an agreed statement of the case or by suggesting the appointment of a Cabinet committee, the issues are fairly and fully stated. They can also ensure that the ultimate decision is communicated to all those ministers, whether members of the Cabinet or not, who may be interested and especially those who may be required to take positive action under the decision. Between them, of course, the officers of the secretariat are bound to get early warning of departmental squabbles of inconsistencies and they can, through the Secretary, make suggestions to the Prime Minister for the appointment of an interdepartmental committee or for the inclusion of the item on the agenda of one of the regular formal Cabinet meetings.

From these short sketches you might perhaps assume that the truth lies in a combination of the two theories. But even that would be a good deal short of the whole truth.

You will remember that I mentioned the very wide control the Treasury exercises in matters of expenditure, including the remuneration and conditions of service of government servants. I also referred to its recognized functions of coordination and to the fact that its permanent secretary has a special position in relation to the Prime Minister who, as you all know, is First Lord of the Treasury, whereas the Chancellor of the Exchequer is only the Second Lord. Now it will be obvious that the power of the purse is likely to be one of the most frequent occasions of dispute between government departments. And in this sphere one party to the quarrel is always the Treasury. Moreover, in the course of the long series of arguments, one of the Treasury aims must be to ensure that there is as little waste and overlapping as possible between departments, and that different departments pay the same for the same services. It can easily be understood then how potent an instrument the Treasury is in forcing matters which require coordination up to the final seat of executive authority—viz. the Cabinet. At the present moment the Permanent Secretary of the Treasury is the titular Secretary to the Cabinet as well and as he is, on top of all this, recognized as the permanent head of the civil service, it can be imagined how important a place he fills in our system. In his single Pooh-Bah-ish person, all three of the co-ordinating agencies are subsumed.

The danger in our country is not that there should be too little coordination but that there should be too much. Nevertheless, the system works well as a whole. Whether it would work as well in a country which has a federal structure and where the executive and legislative branches are sharply separated, a country, moreover, which has not so highly developed a theory of collective responsibility, I do not know. Obviously coherence is greatly facilitated where there is a Cabinet, jointly and severally responsible to a legislature in which nevertheless it can be reasonably assured of integral approval for its policy by the ordinary working of party loyalty and an assured majority. And perhaps that is enough of what has become a portentously long afterthought.

11

THE FOREIGN SERVICE

BY E. L. WOODWARD

IN THE year 1828 Henry Edward Fox, son of Lord and Lady Holland, and a young man in his twenty-seventh year, was trying to find something to do. He decided upon the diplomatic service. Whereupon his mother wrote to him: "You are very sensible in looking for occupation. A life of *désœuvrement* must be dreadful, and with your talents for writing, quite mortifying." Lady Holland then came down to hard facts. "It is in this precarious state of the government advisable to *secure* something, though it may only be made the means of barter and exchange. Lisbon is now made up. . . . The personal character of the Chef is not such as would make him pleasant to you. That for which we hope to attain, Sir William A'Court [Ambassador to Russia], will be just what you wish as a school in which to learn your business. . . . I should myself have wished Vienna, but your Papa says you particularly dislike the Austrians, and besides it is overrun with Wellesleys in the Chancellerie, who view others with jealousy. . . . Munich is not a bad place . . . but be assured the crack thing for acquirement and real business is A'Court. Stockholm is very disagreeable and inferior in all ways. Madrid has only young Bosanquet; Mr. Gordon not being yet moving from Rio. Otherwise *that* would have been pleasant, barring that the climate kills." Then came a word of admonition: "I only do hope now that you have engaged in this career, you will continue and not give the world the appearance of such fickleness as is always a discredit."

There you have the old English diplomatic service. It was by no means as absurd as it sounds. It included men like Lord

Stratford de Redcliffe and Lord Lyons. Such people were the agents of British policy in times which were not as easy as they appear in retrospect. Their judgment of affairs, their cynical worldly wisdom, their sureness of touch, and indeed their sureness of themselves, served their country well, though often to the exasperation of foreigners. These milords knew little of trade or manufacture,[1] but more than is sometimes supposed of high financial and economic policy. They moved in the narrowest social and governmental circles. They did not dream of learning languages like Russian or Turkish. It would never occur to them that some of God's noblest creatures might not even be Englishmen.

To what extent had the position changed in a hundred years? What is the position now? In 1928 the British foreign service was in a state of transition. Recruitment by competitive examination among nominated candidates had long been in force, but the examination was not overdifficult and the field of candidates limited firstly by the requirement of a private income of $2,500 a year, and secondly by the fact that, apart from the hurdle of nomination, no young man was likely to enter the service unless he enjoyed the kind of life which he would have to lead in it. This diplomatic life was less magnificent than in Lady Holland's time, but there was still a great deal of gold plate about it. Everywhere, and especially in the important posts, personality counted for more than technical equipment. In the three great monarchies of Austria Hungary, Germany, and Russia, and hardly less in Spain and Italy, the way of doing things was as important as the thing done, and an ambassador had always to watch his step. For different reasons the British ambassador at Washington for years on end had to behave like a cat walking on hot bricks. The ambassadors of 1928 did not know very much more than their predecessors of 1828 about

[1] About 1846 the British ambassador at Madrid explained with a certain condescending pity the *maladresse* of his French colleague by the fact that this unfortunate man had "spent his early days in a counting-house."

trade and commerce, but once again they were not as ignorant of the main lines of economic policy as is believed, for example, by people who have never read the dispatches from the embassy at Constantinople.

Important reforms—the abolition of the income qualification and the amalgamation of the foreign office and the diplomatic service—were carried out after the first world war. These changes were necessary owing to changed conditions in England and elsewhere. The leftward movement of opinion at home considered that the foreign service of a democracy ought not to be staffed by a small class of rich men. Conditions outside Great Britain were now very different. The great European monarchies had vanished; the grand dukes, the archdukes and the high mightinesses no longer ruled the roost. Furthermore political questions required more detailed knowledge. The new League of Nations might even supersede diplomacy, and the League was officered by civil servants while its meetings were attended by politicians more often than by professional diplomats.

These changes in 1918-1919 obviously could not have their full effect at once. In 1939 the ambassadors belonged to the old regime. Lower down in the service, however, the results of reform were already being felt. During the period between the two wars there was very great interest in foreign affairs among young men at the universities; the foreign service, freed from the old restrictions, attracted a higher percentage of ability than before 1914. During these inter-war years the foreign service secured its full share of the really first-class men entering the service of the Crown.

Even if there had been no war in 1939, the service would have changed its character very markedly by 1950, but it would still have been limited to some extent by the traditions of a single social milieu. If it had ceased to be the preserve of the old upper class, it recruited few young men who did not belong by family or education to the upper level of the professional middle class and the standard of ability had risen because, for a number of reasons good and bad, this class up to the present has contained a very high percentage of the brains of the country. The second world war pushed much further the changes accelerated by the first war. In England the leftward movement of opinion has gained greatly in momentum. There is a much stronger feeling that the representation and exposition of British policy abroad, together with the other duties of the foreign service, ought not to be solely or almost entirely in the hands of one social class; some "left-wingers" indeed have shown almost morbid fears of the world on this point. It is also clear that the need for *savoir-faire* and experience, though still considerable, is not of the kind familiar to Lady Holland and her friends.[2] Above all, in England as elsewhere, the business of the foreign service has altered in character. This business covers a much wider field largely owing to the immense increase in the functions of governments. Foreign affairs are matters dealt with directly between government and government. If governments make large purchases of raw commodities and raw materials, if they control means of transport and can decide freight charges, if they own all the mines of a country, if they engage in selling steel, then a thousand and one questions which were once settled between individuals or between large industrial concerns are decided in negotiations between government and government. Moreover the position is not very dissimilar if the relations between government and industry are reversed, and if, instead of government controlling great industry, great industry controls the government. In either case an ambassador has to know something about the importance of particular industries in the economy and politics of the country to which he is sent.

Laissez-faire, as understood by our great-great-grandfathers, is now impossible and, in view of the direct intrusion of eco-

[2] Newman's well-known definition of a gentleman is still a good summary of the qualities desirable in an ambassador.

nomics—and very complicated economics at that—into politics, it is necessary for the efficiency of a foreign service that its members should understand the economic structure of the modern world and should be able to discern interests outside the circles of diplomatic capitals. As far as Great Britain is concerned this new demand fits in with the other democratic demand for widening the basis of recruitment because the new subjects required are not those humanistic studies in which Oxford and Cambridge and the leading English "public schools"[3] had a predominance.

At this point, however, I should say that, if it is generally accepted that the functions of the foreign service have widened, and that its members should be drawn from more than one class in English society, there is also a recognition of the fact that the service needs a special *expertise*. Those who have observed the service at close quarters are perhaps more aware of this need than the public in general which is apt to be unduly contemptuous of the old diplomacy and, by analogy, of the old diplomats. A foreign service differs from a home civil service in many important respects. If every service requires loyalty and an *esprit de corps* among its members, a foreign service can be more quickly run without it. The members of a diplomatic mission, living in a certain isolation abroad, must have the knack of getting on well with one another as well as with foreigners. Easy relations are not created but they are facilitated by social equality. Diplomacy is not a celibate profession; men marry as a rule from their own social class and in a foreign service their wives are not just lost in a distant suburb and not known to their colleagues or to their colleagues' wives. Or again, bad temper is a nuisance in any government office; it is fatal to a diplomat. Finally, keeping one's nerve in a crisis is even more essential in diplomacy than in home administration. There are also many minor posts where the holder is living

---

[3] The American term would be "private schools."

under conditions of great loneliness as well as under climatic conditions of an unpleasant kind.

Personal acceptability and a certain roundedness of behavior are not all. There are intellectual qualities more needed in diplomacy than in other branches of the public service. For example: especial quickness and sensitivity in the matter of exact statement. By exact statement I do not mean understatement. Understatement has been almost a traditional British weapon. It is a valuable weapon if only because it gives extra vehemence to strong language when such language is necessary. What I have in mind, however, is extreme precision of statement in conversation, and here again I think not of the precision of a judge but of a man trained to think very quickly how his words might be twisted or misinterpreted. It is an interesting thing that negotiations carried out in person by British politicians are rarely as successful as those conducted by professional diplomats. When Lord Haldane, one of the cleverest men of his time, and a trained lawyer as well as a logician, went to Germany a year or so before 1914, his visit was a failure and led to misunderstanding because the Germans supposed him to mean something which he had not intended to convey. When Lord Halifax visited Berlin in 1937, a similar misunderstanding took place. It requires a long training to be able to say what you mean—and perhaps to say it by not saying it—without giving an impression that you mean more—or less—than you have said. This training can be imparted more easily by the kind of schooling envisaged by Lady Holland than by courses on economic geography or the trade cycle.

In a word, diplomacy is an art and not a branch of mechanics; it requires a certain method of approach to questions, a mixture of intelligence and intuition. Perhaps I can illustrate what I mean from my own experience. It has happened that since the autumn of 1939 I have been doing in the British foreign office work of a kind which has given me a very good opportunity of seeing the service as a whole. When I had been in the office a few months, one of the ablest senior members of the staff said to me: "What do you think of the place?" I said: "Well, it seems to me rather amateur." He answered: "That is just what I thought when I came into it. After a time I changed my mind." After a time I too changed my mind. I found that what I took to be a happy-go-lucky hit or miss attitude was nothing of the kind. There was—in my opinion—not enough detailed knowledge, and the reason for this was mainly that the office was—and is—understaffed, with the result that no one had time to acquire the kind of knowledge which seems to me necessary, but the method of approach to questions was very far from amateur or hand to mouth. Indeed, if I go back to the definition of diplomacy as an art, I should say that the artistic element consisted largely in sensitiveness to the color and shape of things and in extreme skill in concentrating upon relevant and essential facts.

This power of concentration upon essentials has been one of the historic marks of a small governing class. Can such *expertise* in any branch of the art of government be continued? One of the most remarkable achievements of the English in the nineteenth century was to devise a mode of education ("system" is hardly the word for it) which gave to the English upper middle class some of the traditional qualities of an old governing aristocracy (for all its merits German education never succeeded in doing this). Can the process be continued among wider circles of English society, or will the butter be too thinly spread? Here we have the problem as it affects the selection of men for the foreign service. It is, in different forms, also the problem which faces the universities which educate the young men likely to be chosen for a foreign service. We have to choose from much wider circles in society a foreign service which has to perform many more varied functions and requires more technical knowledge and which must yet possess nearly all the qualities of the diplomatic service of earlier times.[4]

[4] I have not touched upon another important change in the conditions

British Foreign Service

The British government had these problems in mind when in 1943 it issued a parliamentary paper on "Proposals for the Reform of the Foreign Service." From the point of view of recruitment and training the main feature of the plan is that candidates will be chosen after a preliminary competitive entrance test designed so that it can be taken without special study, followed by a training period abroad at the expense of the state. Candidates who are successful in this entrance test, which in normal cases will be of a standard requiring a university degree, will be given studentships for eighteen months in order to learn two languages in the countries where they are spoken, to study history and economics and to "acquire the necessary familiarity with life in countries other than their own." They will then be given another examination and, if successful, will become probationary members of the foreign service subject to one year's work in Great Britain. Half of this year will be spent in the foreign office. The other half will be spent in the study of economic, industrial, and social questions in other government departments dealing with these affairs and in visiting centers of industry or in other suitable ways. The plan may put too much emphasis upon economics and too little on politics, but in other respects it is to be welcomed. It is, of course, based upon the methods of selection for the Indian civil service. It tries to solve the problem of widening the social field of selection by putting the first entrance test immediately after the end of the average university course. The avenue to a university degree is now open in England to any boy of good ability, thus the question of means will not limit candidates. Moreover, the year and a half of study abroad is a modern substitute—at the expense of the state—for the grand tour which gave

of the foreign service: the relation between the politician who comes and goes and the high official who is always there. The increase in the complexity of business has given the official certain advantages which, for example, the senior members of the foreign office staff did not possess in their relations with Lord Palmerston or Lord Salisbury.

the young milords of a century and more ago a chance of learning something about the world.

Since this paper on foreign office reform was issued another
experiment has been tried. The purpose of this experiment has
been to deal with the special problem of the "veterans," or in
the English term, ex-servicemen, whose education was inter-
rupted at various stages by the war and whom it would be unfair to select by competitive examination, because they would
be competing at such different levels. During the war much use
was made of psychological tests in the selection of officers for
the armed forces. The results of selection by a board which included experts and non-experts were in general most satisfactory. The plan has now been extended to the selection of
civil servants. The method adopted is "to bring together a
fairly large number of candidates in a residential center" (in
other words, a country house) "where they spend several days
under constant observation, both as individuals and in groups,
by a team of trained observers representing both the 'employer'
interest and expert psychological opinion. The simple argument in favor of this system is that three days observation of a
candidate's fitness under these conditions is likely to afford a
prospective employer a better idea of the candidate's fitness
for any given job than a half hour's interview in which he can
be judged only as an individual and not as a member of a
group." The reports of the board of observers are not final.
They are submitted to the civil service commissioners who lay
them before a final selection board. This board places the candidates in an order of merit. Without discussing the experiment
in detail, I can say that neither I nor anyone I know has observed in candidates who have taken part in it a sense that it
was not fair. I have seen a very sharp criticism of some of the
questions put by one of the psychologists, but this criticism did
not apply to the general experiment as such. All the candidates
to whom I have spoken enjoyed themselves, though one of them
said to me that, while he found the tests entertaining, he did

not think that they were very relevant to a judgment upon his capacity for being a good ambassador.

The civil service commissioners—of whom, if I may be allowed to say so, I have a very high opinion—are not committed to a continuance of this system after the present special circumstances have ceased to apply. The system is very expensive and I am inclined to think that, just as there are "cramming" establishments highly skilled in forecasting the type of question—and answer—to be expected in a written examination, there will soon come into existence special "crammers" for these psychological tests. The selecting body may therefore find their task more difficult because the prudent candidate will have given himself a good deal of practice in the more specialized tests to which he is likely to be submitted. Nevertheless, I believe that this system in some form or other has come to stay and I am sure that it is better than the old type of *viva voce*.

Whatever the method of selecting them, these candidates for the foreign service and other branches of administration are likely to have been educated at the universities. What ought we to teach them? The problem hardly arises with the small handful of men of the highest ability. Luckily we cannot do them much harm, and we may do them good if we allow them as much freedom as possible. No government service can be made up entirely of first-class men—there are not enough of them to go round; the efficiency of a service is finally determined not by the stars but by the average second class. Here we can do a great deal. As far as English experience goes, I might sum up our problem by saying that, roughly, there are two schools of thought: one school inclines to push vocational training back into the university years and to encourage specialization in the social sciences—economics, public administration, the history and working of institutions, and so on. The other school holds that our business is not necessarily to give men an introduction to the practical matters with which they will have to deal later on but to provide them with the best kind of mental background and training. It may well be that the best mental training is to be gained from subjects which have nothing directly to do with the social and economic or administrative problems of today. Some people think that the study of Greek and Latin, especially in the form which these studies have taken at Oxford and Cambridge, provides the best training. This is not merely the opinion of classical teachers who might be said to have a vested interest in their subjects. The head of one of the largest business concerns in Great Britain (with branches all over the world) said some time ago in my hearing that his firm found that for all posts requiring capacities above the routine level the best material came from Oxford and Cambridge and that on the whole he thought that the old Greek and Latin discipline was the best preparation for a business career.

It has certainly been true in the past that a classical training has supplied the English administrative services with candidates of a very high caliber, and the list of great administrators who have had this training is sufficient to dispose of the neo-obscurantism which has no room for the masterpieces of ancient literature and regards composition into Latin and Greek as outmoded pedantry. On the other hand, from the fact that the classical discipline has produced remarkable results it does not follow that other disciplines are not capable of producing results as good or better. Moreover the primacy of classical studies in times past is not really relevant to the discussion because the new subjects had not been molded to a form suited to make them a vehicle for general education. In any case, whether we think it a good or bad thing, the position in England now is that, except for a minority, the classical discipline cannot be made a *sine qua non* because it requires a long grinding at school, and this preliminary work at Latin and Greek is unlikely to be possible at the average state school which does not possess the necessary staff. If therefore you insist upon a knowledge of Latin and Greek you are limiting entry into your civil service to candidates from one social class or, more accurately, from those schools (not always confined to one social class) where Latin and Greek are taught.

Hence in practice we in England are faced with the fact that for the greater number of entrants into our foreign or home civil services we must provide something other than the old form of training, but if there is a conservatism which refuses to face this fact, there is a "progressivism"—to use an unpleasing term—which refuses to see that the classical discipline was elaborated after centuries of experience by able teachers and that, for obvious reasons, the educational value of the newer subjects is by no means well established. Once again, I do not mean to suggest that these new subjects cannot form as good a basis of education as Greek and Latin; the point is that at present they are not very satisfactory for our purpose and our problem is how to make them into a vehicle for general education.

We have not yet solved this problem in Great Britain. Educational institutions of all kinds in the United States have done more organized thinking about it partly because with them the problem has come up more urgently for solution. I have read with the greatest interest a few of the reports of committees at American universities where the methods of teaching contemporary subjects have been carefully reviewed. I am sure that we in England have a great deal to learn from these reports. What, if anything, can we provide in return?

I cannot speak for English universities—still less for Scottish universities—in general and all that I can tell you about one university—Oxford—is tentative. We put less emphasis upon the lecture system; we feel perhaps, that, as with other types of sleeping draught, an overdose kills the patient. It may be that we give too much weight to our final examinations—a test of 10 to 12 3-hour papers—but we think that this final examination should be a test of a man's reading and development over the whole period of his residence. We are, however, very uncertain about the content of our syllabus in modern subjects. To some extent our uncertainty is due merely to backwardness in recognizing these subjects. My own subject of international relations, for example, is still barely accepted as an academic study. I could make a long story of the things which any American professor of the subject would regard as essential to the organization of his work and which I do not possess (a secretary, one or more research assistants, a special library, even a set of maps). On the other hand there are fields in which we have made great progress on the side of research (economics, public administration, the study of institutions), although we are still undecided about the best way of grouping them for the purpose of teaching. At Oxford we have been trying to combine modern philosophy, economics, and politics (including history) into a single main 3-year course, but each of the three subjects has been and still is jostling for position and, on the whole, the philosophers and economists are tougher men than the politicians and historians whose subjects tend to come off worst in the struggle. The course is very popular, but not many of those who teach it are satisfied with it as it now is. Speaking for myself, I should say that what we are trying to do is to recover something which will give to the undergraduate a sense of form. This sense of form goes very deep. To my mind it can be communicated only through the study of the great masters of literature. I believe also that it cannot be gained without some effort at least comparable with the effort required to translate English into Latin and I do not think that we can get the best out of the average student (a different process from putting the best into him) until we have installed French—not German, and not English—into the place once occupied by Latin in our educational scheme. I say this, however, when I am several thousand miles away from those of my colleagues who are less concerned with form and more with content than I am, and who do not share my uneasiness about the jargon and the second-rateness of so many of our textbooks and monographs on contemporary political and economic subjects. Nevertheless, if I am old-fashioned, I am unrepentant in holding that a civil servant—whether in the foreign or home service —should learn at the university to see men as the great masters have seen them. If he does not learn this lesson at the university, he is unlikely to learn it elsewhere, and least of all when he has joined the ranks of the "twice-born" bureaucracy and, a fully informed modern civil servant among other fully informed modern civil servants, is climbing the ladder of official promotion.

12

AN AMERICAN VIEW OF THE
BRITISH EXPERIENCE

BY PAUL APPLEBY

THE essays of Sir James Grigg and Professor Woodward provide expositions of what already has been done in the United Kingdom. Naturally, then, they have given a minimum of attention to appraising the record, and have had little to say about changes that may be required in order to meet the needs of a changing social order.

Perhaps all of us would agree that the British system has produced up to now many more good generalists than are produced by American educational and selection methods. Here, I think, we produce many more and, within certain limits, abler specialists. But the limitations of our specialists are usually very marked. We must conclude that the British emphasis on broad preparation has much significance.

The two essays have that excellent use of language which is characteristic of the British university man, and of the British civil servant, one which most Americans can but envy. I find many phrases to applaud, phrases such as these: "Seeing men as the great masters have seen them"; "a sense of form," "ability to deal with men," and "men given to action."

All of these things reinforce a judgment I am sure we all have had in our dealings with the British government as we encountered an exceptionally high order of intelligence, extraordinary intergovernmental communication and general teamwork, and urbanity.

But if one must peer critically into these two stories of the British experience, certain questions do arise. The effort must be to try to appraise this experience in terms of applicability

180

elsewhere and in the future. One may feel as I do about the close kinship of our societies, and feel that the British society is the most stable and surely democratic society in the present world, and still have some doubts about the future adequacy in the United Kingdom or the transferability to us of large parts of this British experience.

For both our countries—indeed, increasingly for all nations— the emphasis on generalists is valid and transferable. The more complex the world becomes, the more specialist work in more fields, the more difficult becomes the task of synthesis. Here in America our attention has gone rather exclusively to specialization. In consequence, our most tragic governmental inadequacies are in levels analogous to those occupied by the British "administrative class."

The most serious questions about the British experience, however, are suggested by that very phrase, "administrative class." The British still accept the idea of a special "class" or a class system with much more equanimity than we do. We accept here perpendicular class lines occasionally, as in the case of the "professional class" in our civil service, but not horizontal class lines. I wonder whether we aren't moving a little toward the British situation, and whether the British are not moving a good deal toward ours.

At all events, I find in these essays, quite naturally, a good deal of the reflection of a scene not like ours, and certainly not altogether like the British social scene of the future. The country-house week-end method of passing upon eligibility to the Civil Service Club, for example, seems to me not at all applicable here. I wonder whether it, or anything much like it, can long continue to be useful or acceptable over there, even though for a while it may have beneficial results.

The "ability to get on well with one another" emphasized by Professor Woodward is conceived of in terms of "social equality." I wonder how really well equipped for "getting on well with foreigners," or simply for "getting on well with citizens" are staffs recruited according to such criteria.

At another place Professor Woodward says, "This power of concentration upon essentials has been one of the historic marks of a small governing class." May it not be that the type of education and the methods of selection described by our British friends are adequate only where there is a recognized governing class?

Let me develop this question by asking several others: In a more volatile society, a more rough-and-ready society, a less disciplined society, would the British system of preparation and selection of civil servants succeed nearly as well as it does in Britain? Would the persons so educated and so chosen be in fact as good administrators as they are in the British government? How much of their success has come internationally from the power Britain has had, and how much from the real human understanding and man-to-man effectiveness of the civil servants? How much of their domestic success has come from the fact that the civil servants speak and act in the manner of long-established class authority, and how much from a more generally applicable ability to manage relatively undisciplined social situations?

These questions are not intended to be at all invidious. It is highly important to think earnestly and deeply about the relationship between officials and those for whom and with whom they work in a society increasingly democratic as well as increasingly complex. In government of, by, and for the people there are not only questions of intellectual capacity to consider; there are also very intricate questions of personal effectiveness under popular responsibility. Superiority in ability must be an acceptable, thoroughly considerate, and responsive ability, intimately related to the citizens served. The leftward movement mentioned by both writers is much to be emphasized as we think about developing future leaders. This leftward movement is in part the fruit of a vast scientific and technological advance, and in part a simple fruit of democracy. Granted general franchise and an extension of education, it was inevitable that new requirements for leadership would emerge. It would seem most probable that even sober and stable Britain will become much more volatile, much less simply disciplined.

This social development needs to be thought about in connection with other developments if we are to keep pace with the times. The fields of specialized knowledge and the field of governmental action have so expanded that we cannot afford uncritically to accept old ideas. There must be constant inquiry about what general and broad education will be commensurate with the new content of affairs. Difficult problems in the development of curricula and of material to be used in specific courses must be pondered. The relationship between persons especially equipped for official leadership and the citizens they serve is not something to be treated casually as questions of traditional academic excellence and eligibility for club membership. There is a special element of popular kinship and effectiveness that must be carefully explored.

Both statements on the British experience have assumed a political neutrality of civil servants which, in the way in which it is currently understood in their country, is warranted. Beginning at any moderately acute stage, policy in the United Kingdom does seem always to be reasonably controllable by the political heads of the government. Yet we all know that at less acute stages there are a million and one ways in which administrators and executives determine or influence policy. It is not possible for human organizations to function otherwise. In these matters the question of sensitive kinship with citizens generally is pervasively important. This question has never been adequately considered anywhere. In this respect I am inclined to feel that the American civil service is at least as well adjusted to the American scene as the British service is

Paul Appleby

adjusted to its scene. But in both cases the result is a rather simple product of history, with little aid from scholars.

Sir James seems to imply at one point that anyone who can be outstanding in various general fields of academic learning can—on account of that demonstrated ability—learn also to be a good administrator. If there is any such implication, it should be challenged. Chester Barnard in his Lowell Lectures, "The Functions of the Executive," gives an important discussion of the values ordinarily thought of as intellectual, in the field of socio-dynamics. It *is* the field of socio-dynamics with which administrators have to deal. Both essays, in spite of incidental phrases such as "ability to deal with men" and "men given to action" seem to me not really to be directed very much along the line of those phrases.

Indeed, Sir James Grigg states quite flatly that the ability to manage men, "like most of the really important capacities, can only be acquired by learning to do it in practice." One can agree with this statement and still feel that it begs the question that is the occasion for this series of essays: How can we prepare young men and young women so that they may learn more in practice?

There would appear, then, to be excellent ground for questioning Sir James' disbelief in "institutes or faculties or theoretical courses of public administration." Professor Woodward does question it, and I regard these sentences from his essay as having outstanding significance: "From the fact that the classical discipline has produced remarkable results, it does not follow that other disciplines are not capable of producing results as good or better. Moreover, the primacy of classical studies in times past is not really relevant to the discussion because the new subjects had not been molded to a form suited to make them a vehicle for general education. . . . The point is that at present they are not very satisfactory for our purpose, and our problem is how to make them into a vehicle for general education."

An American View

Professor Woodward goes on to say that more organized thinking has been done about this problem in our country than in his. I believe this to be true, but it seems to me that too little of our thinking has been in terms of making these subjects into "a vehicle for general education." There already is a tendency to make our courses in public administration as narrowly specialized as we make so many of our vocational courses. This is a danger to be found particularly in proposals put forward by good citizens newly aware of our civil service, for a "West Point for civil servants." Our universities should produce young people ready to launch upon careers of public service. But the great effort should be not so much to produce merely persons qualified to get CAF-5 jobs; it should be to produce those potentially qualified to hold CAF-14 and 15 places, and posts even higher not yet established in our classification system or in the public mind as places requiring career public servants.

In this connection a word should be said for recruitment of a fair percentage of our civil servants at stages later than completion of academic work. The next largest body of recruits might well be enrolled at about the ages of twenty-seven and twenty-eight. Provision always should exist for occasional enrichment of the service by bringing in still older persons at still higher levels. Until recently recruitment of this kind for our foreign service has been illegal, and I believe that no other single factor has been equally harmful to the quality of that service.

This, finally, leads to an observation concerning Professor Woodward's emphasis on elements differentiating the selection of foreign service personnel from civil service proper. It seems to me that the point is inconsistent with the emphasis both essays give to general qualifications. Differences between departments, bureaus, and work locations do exist, of course, but these are differences that can best be adjusted to in practice. Actually, there is warrant for raising critical questions

Paul Appleby

about the relative efficiency in public service of special corps organizations. All departments, all bureaus, all disciplines, all skills, and all localities tend to resist top-level general direction and coordination on the ground that they are "different." Yet it is this relating of "different" things to the totality of things in application to a whole people that is the essence of that synthesis which is public administration.

PART V

THE ROLE OF UNIVERSITY EDUCATION

✦ 13 ✦

A FIRST VIEW:
THE UNIVERSITY-WIDE APPROACH

BY JOHN M. GAUS

A DISCUSSION of the basic theme of this volume is most appropriate. After the many events relevant to the theme during the past quarter century, and the urgency of the public business that confronts our governments, a fresh appraisal is needed. The basis for such an appraisal lies in part in the variety of previous studies, reports, conferences, and experiences of institutions concerned with government personnel. Such studies as George Graham's *Education for Public Administration* and the experience of such institutions as the National Institute of Public Affairs are certainly pertinent. Also basic to such an appraisal are the findings of such conferences as the Princeton conference called by the Public Administration Clearing House in 1935 and the University of Minnesota Conference on University Training for the National Service of 1931.

In the "Resolutions and Recommendations of the Conference" held at Princeton in 1935, there is, in the concluding paragraph of the section on "Pre-Entry Academic Preparation" the statement that "the Conference feels that inasmuch as problems of preparation concern the whole university and touch upon so many phases of educational policy, anything less than a university-wide approach to the problems would be unsatisfactory." Professor William Anderson, Minnesota Conference in 1931, remarked that "the greatest need at the present time is that the universities shall understand the problems of the public service, and that contacts shall be established between those officers of the government who recruit and employ men, and those officers of the universities who

189

have charge of special types of training." I quote these observations because I believe they are pertinent today, and therefore will support my referring to questions that are the subject matter of other essays in this volume.

To give usable meaning to the term "public service" we must turn to the central task of classification. It is on this point that discussion of the topic before the first world war—and it is useful to recall that there was a general interest in the question at once stimulated by and reflected in the establishment of the Training School for the Public Service in New York and of a committee of the American Political Science Association, to cite two of several examples—differs somewhat from the emphasis usefully introduced at the Minnesota Conference and subsequently at other conferences at Princeton and elsewhere. The earlier discussion could not attain the sharpness of focus on definable objectives of classified positions for which educational policies could be prepared which it is now more nearly possible to obtain—even if incompletely. The classification of public positions was just beginning; the establishing of regular methods of recruitment, based upon specifications of positions indicating qualifications, and administered by personnel with some educational and experience qualifications, was much less advanced. Even today progress in these essentials is too little known among university departments and colleges, and in the public generally, and spiritless yearnings for something "like the English have" too often reflect the extent of appreciation of the complex questions that open before us. The Minnesota. Conference brought a healthy, open-air concreteness to this discussion. It came after the classification movement had made gains, including the passage of the national Classification Act, and experience with classification systems was accumulating and more readily available for comparative analysis. Connections were being established between the growing number of students of public administration and the leagues of municipalities and organizations of a professional type—soon to be facilitated by the recently established Public Administration Clearing House, which was to call the Princeton Conference four years later.

Acquaintance with the range of employments in the public service represented in classifications of various jurisdictions supported the findings I have quoted above, as well as William Anderson's further comment in 1931 that "in a broad sense, all university education is training for the national service. Without fully realizing and largely without intending it, colleges and universities have been supplying national, state, and local governments with their specialists, scientists, and professional workers." The focusing of attention on the fact of a great variety of public services, instead of a single vocational entity dubbed "the public service," has made a more useful attack on the question possible, for it has facilitated comparative and cumulative studies at many places. It is significant that in this volume are chapters assigned to discuss single and more sharply defined fields within the public services. And the same process of exploration of concrete types of public employment has brought us to a recognition of the different nature of the problem of relating education to the public services in the different levels of government. Thus the absence of a single center for recruiting for various municipal employments, coupled with the operation of residence rules, creates a very different problem than exists in recruiting for a classified position in the national civil service, where applicants may be taking, at the same time in many places throughout the country, an examination on materials which could be studied at hundreds of educational institutions.

In thus noting a change in the treatment of our topic in the direction of a more concrete defining of objectives by means of classification of employments, we may also usefully recall that it was possible for the Princeton Conference to devote one half of its findings to "In-Service or Post-Entry Training." The development, as a part of sound personnel policy, of such types

191

of education, and the recognition of the desirable goal of continuous education, modifies the formulation of policies of pre-entry education. As in-service training and adult education programs generally develop and improve, the universities are better able to determine and fulfill their own appropriate task.

These and other changes in the conditions affecting education for the public service are reflected by (and in part influenced by) the various experiments which have been initiated since the first world war, some of them building on the earlier institution of the Training School for Public Service at the New York Bureau of Municipal Research. Progress has been made in the clarifying of objectives through the experience of these educational programs, through surveys such as those by the Commission on Public Service Personnel, by Lambie for the Public Administration Clearing House, by Graham for the Committee on Public Administration of the Social Science Research Council, and by the President's Committee on Civil Service Improvement; through the classification and training work of personnel recruitment agencies; and through the work of individual scholars, recorded in articles and books of which the writings, for example, of Leonard White, Lewis Meriam, Dwight Waldo, Arthur Macmahon, Paul Appleby, and Robert Walker may be cited as illustrative. Even the catastrophe of the depression, by challenging youth to reconsider vocational objectives and stimulating new forms of government activity, must be considered as a major influence in the change in the setting of our problem. Events in Europe brought to us scholars and administrators who could enrich, as Arnold Brecht, for example, has done, our knowledge of other systems; and the increase in research in comparative government by our own scholars, aided by Social Science Research Council and other fellowships continues a process of exploration begun earlier by Henry Adams, Dorman Eaton, and Robert Moses.

Where do we now stand as to objectives—that is, most immediately and concretely, as to the classification of the public service? How do the educational programs that have been developed relate to these objectives?

Very broadly considered, our processes of government require participation of a large proportion of our population as voters; a smaller number as active workers in parties and civic groups concerned with public policies; a yet smaller number as elected legislators; and, finally, a small group of elected executives. All but the last of these are employed in the more general policy process and as part-time workers. In addition to these groups, who are often (except, perhaps the last) not thought of as a part of the general category "public service," there is the large group of generally full-time government employees, including the heads of departments, and the workers in substantive fields such as the protection of health or the construction of highways. But finally, in addition to these, two other types of positions have gradually been discerned as necessary. In the terms usefully defined and employed by Leonard White, they may here be referred to as auxiliary service and general staff personnel, including some types of positions not ordinarily found in the traditional substantive employments. Thus the administration of budget and personnel activities as an aid both to substantive departments and political chiefs has emerged only in recent decades, and the positions required are consequently of recent establishment. As functions and the relations of levels and agencies have increased and grown more complex, and social policy more difficult, the need for unified treatment of preparing policies and executing them has brought the unofficial and then the official general staff function and positions into existence.

Now much of the more overt and the newer programs of education for the public service have been pointed to these auxiliary types of functions and positions—partly because advances in governmental research were making clear the urgent need that existed. The general staff type of function and position, less clearly defined and as yet rarely provided for in normal recruitment schemes, is nevertheless frequently lurking in the background of our thought when we consider the relation of universities to the public service. At that point, perhaps, we are influenced by some aspects of the role of the British administrative class, by the example of the British Cabinet Secretariat, and by the kind of service which should be provided by what the administrative assistants to the President, to governors, mayors, and city managers might become—assuming that such positions could be defined and made a more regular part of the general personnel arrangements. But the University of Minnesota Conference pioneered in showing that such positions as these auxiliary and general staff types were relatively few compared to the great range and variety of positions of a substantive type. These were in the public service, to be sure—engineers of all sorts, doctors, chemists, stenographers, janitors, literally hundreds of different vocations; but the primary fact about them was not the fact of jurisdiction, of being in the government service (so far as educational policy is concerned), but the nature of the vocation whether in government or any other type of employment. With rare exceptions there was not, for example, a special kind of chemistry peculiar to government as against a private concern, to be studied in the course in chemical engineering. To be sure, there were secondary considerations created by the fact of employment in government which might usefully be considered in the educational process; but even there a limiting factor existed in the fact that one could rarely foresee during the period in the professional school whether one would be employed by a department of health or by a chemical manufacturing company or as a free lance consultant.

Hence, the deduction drawn at the Minnesota Conference, and reiterated at the Princeton Conference, concerning the university-wide nature of the problem of educating for the public service. Every conceivable type of training offered in a university would have its graduates liable at some time to be employed in government. Nor was this all; they might also find themselves increasingly responsible not only for the substantive problems of their fields, but also, with promotions, some of them might acquire extensive general administrative responsibilities. Macmahon's pioneer studies of the careers of bureau chiefs conclusively demonstrated this point, and made all thinking concerning education for the public service worthless unless it were taken into account, and Lewis Meriam has made this fact of the size, scope, and nature of the substantive employments in government the cornerstone of his useful writings and observations.

But let us carry this diagnosis of the tradition and practice of substantive careers a step further in the changing setting of American life of the past quarter-century. The increase in functions and scope of government, the complexities and variables that confront those responsible for industry, commerce, agriculture, and the professions, the evolution of ideas of the nature of our systems and processes such as those of Frederick Taylor and his disciples, for example, have all conspired to emphasize the institutional aspects of every occupation, regardless of its jurisdiction. Thus there has emerged not only the problem of education for the public service, but some more adequate place in professional or vocational training of every sort for an introduction to its ecological setting and public aspects. Medical schools have mothered schools of public health, and debate inclusion in their own programs of some consideration of "medical economics"; one need not apply the point to other professions and their schools. How far such considerations can find a place in the crowded professional school curricula, how adequate such specialized approaches to larger public questions are, whether it would be better to look to the pre-professional years and courses for an introduction to the society and its problems so far as educational institutions can provide such introduction, how added course content is to be reconciled with the value of shortening the period of time and the financial burden required for professional or vocational training—these are the resultant and urgent questions. Here it is relevant to point out that these issues reinforce the wisdom of making education for the public service a search that is university-wide, for having any unit established to foster such education, one which supplements, stimulates, and cooperates with all the other substantive units of the university even if it also has its own program of training for those relatively few types of positions which do not fall within traditional vocational fields. We take for granted the fact of great variety of circumstances among our educational institutions. Courses available, personality of teachers, physical location, and other factors will properly affect its policies in this, as other, fields. But where there is any considerable range of vocational courses such as law, medicine, engineering, commerce, and agriculture, for example, it would seem that a very substantial educational task of any unit concerned with the public service will be educating those schools as to the specific opportunities in public service, to mention only the most obvious and elementary phase of its work—a phase in which there is increasing assistance from recruiting authorities and procedures.

Perhaps it may not seem appropriate to consider the training for public service appropriately to be attempted in the university for that largest group mentioned in the effort at classification above—the voters, party and civic workers, legislators, and other elective officials whom we may presume to be political leaders. Here again prediction in college years can only safely extend to the fact that most of our students ought at some future time, at least, to be voters! There is a general assumption, by many, that they constitute, also, the potential political leaders—the term leadership, indeed, often hovers about such discussions. The cynical might express doubts, based upon recollections of college reunion talk, or doctrines of economic determinism. Perhaps Mr. Belloc has expressed the most poignant view in his poem of college recollection entitled "Dedicatory Ode":

> But something dwindles, oh! my peers,
> And something cheats the heart and passes,
> And Tom that meant to shake the years
> Has come to merely rattling glasses.

But we cannot afford to leave the question there. Here again the findings of the earlier Princeton conference are instructive. Mention was made (1) of "the general concepts of citizenship"; of "insight into the kind of social structure in which government operates; the social forces which furnish the major drives in contemporary society; and trends in contemporary economic and social life; (2) a range of knowledge relating to the structure; and the principal operations of administration, especially staff operations." These were viewed as "desirable . . . that students who contemplate entering the public service in any classification . . . will find it advantageous as undergraduates to acquire." May we move beyond this cautious expression, and assert that whether the student "contemplates entering the public service" shall be interpreted as every student, since all will be voters, occupiers of space in city or country, and inevitable participants in their vocation in the making of decisions of public consequences? The program of education in citizenship initiated by William Mosher at Syracuse University, that now under development under the leadership of Robert Walker at Kansas State College, that developed by Garfield Jones at the University of Toledo, the comparative studies in civic education instituted by Charles Merriam, illustrate the recognition in this quarter century of a responsibility for re-thinking the part to be played by the universities in civic education; a committee on undergraduate instruction of the American Political Science Association includes in its report some treatment of the topic.

Nor is the education of the student who is in future bound

to be a participant in the public service as defined above exclusively a matter of formal curriculum and instruction. Already and without special stimulus students make their way to us for advice, or "just to talk things over," in efforts to integrate all their activities including studies and their participation in the life of the college community, their personal problems, employment, the choice of vocation, the significance of the events of the day, into some more meaningful life. They are, in fact, apprentices, and they seek guiding craftsmen and some more experienced comradeship. Experimentation with systems of counseling, advisorships, and tutorial programs has been marked in the period we are considering. It is sometimes weak on the side of the supply of information that is based upon first-hand experience or acquaintance with the rapidly changing developments in public service. There was a useful attempt, more than fifty years ago, to relate this need among university students to the new urban challenges through the settlement houses. In our period, the development of such a program as that of the National Institute of Public Affairs, and many local programs, illustrate one phase of this desire to relate study to participation.

Progress in defining needs and objectives through more concrete classification of the public service and in educational programs alike point to a clarifying of the substantial responsibilities of the university in education for the public service. Those responsibilities include the fostering of a greater awareness among all the constituent schools of the public aspects of their fields and of specific recruitment opportunities; participation in counseling or advisory services; formulation of curriculum and course provisions whereby the ecology of government and the role of the processes of government are made integral parts of the basic general education of all students; and continuing encouragement of programs at all levels of government whereby methods of recruitment and training will better facilitate our governments in obtaining and making use of the products of our educational institutions. You will recall the sixth of Charles Beard's seven "axioms on public administration"— "Unless the members of an administrative system are drawn from various classes and regions, unless careers are open in it to talents, unless the way is prepared by an appropriate scheme of general education, unless public officials are subjected to internal and external criticism of a constructive nature, then the public personnel will become a bureaucracy dangerous to society and to popular government."

The responsibility for initiating and developing these functions within a university should rest primarily with its department of political science, or government, or politics; and some part of the program requires cooperation through committees or conferences with other units of the university, and with personnel and other governmental and civic bodies with a shared interest in questions of education, recruitment, and post-entry training. To facilitate the most effective discharge of these responsibilities, there may be required, depending on local circumstances, some special operating agency such as a bureau of public administration, especially if there is any extensive program of collaboration in research and consultation with government agencies. If the program is widened to foster the educational preparation of a number of candidates for general staff and auxiliary apprenticeships, whether or not coupled with internships, the organization of a professional school may be appropriate—although it is to be hoped that the fact of education for the public service in other units will not be forgotten. Whether such professional programs should be undertaken in undergraduate years is much debated; it is doubtful if there can be a general answer, divorced from the equipment, location, resources, and personnel of the particular institution. My own present opinion is that there is nothing so perfect about our traditional undergraduate curricula or methods as to warrant a refusal to permit such experimentation in the years in which an undergraduate is working in his major field. You

will recall, too, that Emerson said that "To think about anything is to elevate it."

Among the topics which would form centers or lines of exploration for selected fields of undergraduate concentration
are the emergence of the metropolitan region, the rural and
forest regions as affected by the land use, conservation and related programs of the past fifty years as well as the influence of
international policies, the study of the regions in which particular institutions may be located from the point of view of resources, problems, and institutions, and the study of foreign
regions, somewhat along the lines with which we had some
experience in war programs. The emergence of administration
and of government generally in the evolution of the modern
state, including the more recently recognized problems of
process in policy making and the formulation of public opinion, is an already accepted theme for majors in political science.
All of these topics not only invite but require the making of
programs of study that cut across departmental lines, and relate
technical problems to general social forces; and all of them
stimulate an acquaintance with methods and devices of social
research and self-initiative and discipline. All of them, also,
should make some contribution in the motivation of groups of
students toward a sense of apprenticeship and anticipation of
future participation in public affairs. They would help to prepare the student for those kinds of graduate work which the
various public service training programs have been introducing.

The experience we have had with the various programs initiated in the past twenty-five years seems to me to support the
emphasis I have given here upon a flexible adjustment of university policies to the changing classifications and procedures
in the public service, and to the obligation of all educational
institutions to recognize preparation for participation in public
affairs as an essential part of a general education. And I have
urged that that preparation be reasonably specific—that is, that

it should acquaint the student, so far as content and instruction at least can do, with the ecology and process of government, and the consequent obligation as well as opportunity of the individual citizen. The experience to which I have just referred has happily been varied as to regional location, size and type of institution, interest in level of government, dominant personalities, and philosophy and program. Yet all reflect the closer, more concrete diagnosis of objectives, and most of them a desire to bring the entire institution along in awareness of problem and opportunity. The work is accomplished through different types of organization—a Bureau of Public Administration, as at California; a School of Citizenship and Public Affairs, as at Syracuse; a Public Service Training Center, as at Minnesota; a Southern Regional Training Program, as inaugurated by several universities in the southeast; and Institute of State and Local Government, as at the University of Pennsylvania; and without benefit of title, at so many places, except that of a department. The pioneers, Beard, Gulick, Mosher, Olson, May, Lambie, Herring, Short, Martin, Meriam, and White, to name but a few, have, it will be remembered, not only had to invent new educational programs, but they have participated in the opening up of improved systems of classification and examination. Here the work of Leonard White has been outstanding, for the introduction of a more regular recruiting process and of improved specifications for the junior professional grade would have been unthinkable twenty years ago. It is the more incumbent upon the rest of us, who enjoy the benefits, to do him justice by utilizing the concepts and detailed spade work he has supplied in furthering the evolution of classification and recruitment in these positions of general administration, especially in state and local governments where there is so little even of recognition that such work exists or may be needed.

Not so long ago I was upset by the casual remark of a younger man in the field of public administration to the general effect that of course we can now see how bad the work in personnel administration of the past two decades has been. My inner irritation was such that after I had cooled off a bit I decided that I had grown far older than I had hitherto realized. I had been thinking myself fortunate to be working in a field that was lively, interesting, important, progressive. In all seriousness my younger friend may be right. And I therefore conclude that something of a combination of the Graham Survey and the Commission on Public Service Personnel of the decade of the 'thirties be undertaken for the decade of the 'forties, perhaps under the auspices of the Social Science Research Council. Many of us perhaps become ingrown, and return too often, as I fear I have done here, to hackneyed phrases, and what is worse, tired and exhausted thoughts. It may be that what seems to us, starting out from college about 1915, as so much accomplished in education for the public service, looks to a more recent comer to the field as too little and too late. Maybe the views expressed here as to the necessity for the study of government in any adequate scheme of general liberal education are too subjective and partisan. Doubtless there are deeper problems to be explored. At any rate, I think a fresh exploration and review might be helpful to us all.

And I would charge such a commission or single surveyor with the duty of reporting on at least these matters: the evolution of classification of public service positions, the evolution of systems or recruiting (both at all levels of government), the relation of general administration to careers in substantive fields, the emergence of general staff and auxiliary positions, foreign developments (such as the establishing, for example, of the Scientific Service in Great Britain, or classification, recruitment and education in Russia), the experience with our educational programs, the development of in-service and post-entry and adult education programs, and a sampling of courses in special fields largely if not entirely of a public service type of employment, such as city and regional planning and forestry. Above all, I would hope that the observations of many of those who have gone out from our institutions in the last fifteen years, during which a consciousness of this problem has been stimulated, and have had experience in the public service, would be obtained and appraised. I find them an ample justification for the thought and energy and time that has gone into these developments; they renew my ideas and my enthusiasm. What is more important, upon them, whether in university teaching or in public administration, will fall the responsibility for newer and better policies.

Earlier studies of high school and university enrollments such as those made by the late Dean J. B. Johnston of the University of Minnesota, made clear our losses from the failure of many youth of ability to continue their education. The NYA, ASTP, and now the G.I. programs supply us with evidence that there are sources of ability which we have not sufficiently tapped; and perhaps the most tragic rigidity in our system is that which shuts the Negro from participation in this flow of knowledge and ability into the service to the public. Apart from the absolute case for justice to them, there is the increasingly urgent case of necessity for the United States, in its relations with other peoples, to explore and utilize better within its own immediate family the outlook and insights of its varied peoples. I know of no better setting than that of the university in which these phases of our problem of education for the public service may be explored face to face and with deliberation. Here also a fresh inquiry would have an assignment. What other peoples must attempt at arm's length in distant colonies and at remote frontiers, we—for both good and ill—must do at home.

Our universities (like our nation) are still unfinished and incomplete. We can borrow from abroad, as we have usefully done; but there is a uniqueness even within our regions that

John M. Gaus

has yet fully to be defined and utilized. A great number of
healthy local centers, freely sharing their experiences with one
another, supporting common programs for common advance,
yet intimately reflective of their own local problems and needs,
seems to me to be the teaching of the experience we have had
in this quarter century.

14

A SECOND VIEW:
AN AMERICAN ADMINISTRATIVE CLASS?

BY ROWLAND EGGER

THE preceding essays of this symposium and the discussions developed on the basis of the issues which they join go a long way toward reducing to understandable and manageable proportions the responsibilities of the universities with respect to the future state of health of both the public service and the *corpus politicum* in general. In this particular, among others, the Princeton Bicentennial Conference on university education and the public service has contributed significantly to the charting of what is potentially a courageous and venturesome course for both universities and responsible public officials in meeting the challenge which these troubled years present to political stability and to administrative integrity.

The authors of these essays, as well as the other members of the conference, found a reasonable amount of common ground in their diagnoses of the ills which beset the public service, as well as in the aspects in which the public service has demonstrated unexpected strength and vitality. On the other hand, as the proceedings clearly reveal, sharp differences of opinion were implicit with respect to remedial measures as well as to the causes for the not infrequent manifestations of vigor and good health on the part of the governmental mechanism. Robert Lovett and Sir James Grigg, for example, could probably discuss the merits of open versus closed career service for quite a while without reaching anything like complete accord on the matter, while the views of Arthur Flemming and Struve Hensel with respect to the role of the Civil Service Commission in the recruitment of top-management personnel present certain elements of fundamental incompatibility.

Actually, most of the problems discussed by the conference run to questions of principle entirely outside the field of personnel training and management—to basic issues of social and governmental organization, to social and administrative values, and to intellectual and moral convictions about the shape of things to come. Although the conference topic necessarily directed attention, for the purpose of focusing discussion and sharpening critiques, to a single minimuscular point at which the universities dip into the stream of social action, the portent of the essays and the debate was related primarily to the larger and more fundamental problems of the relationship between higher education and the public service in a free society.

An extremely readable and well-considered summary of the proceedings of the conference has already been written. No good purpose would be served at this time by attempting to redo what has already been done with brilliance and distinction. Moreover, a good many of the problems raised in the course of the conference—important as they are to the effective operation of a competent civil service and dominant though they may be in the environment in which the public servant does his work—are not matters which the universities can influence to any considerable degree. The salary level for top-management positions is a matter for Congress, the state legislatures, and the city councils—not for the university professors. Although we may deplore the shortsightedness of Congress in paying cabinet members less than most city-managers in municipalities of more than 100,000 population receive, and by this fact imposing a corresponding ceiling on salaries of top nonpolitical administrators whose responsibilities are substantially larger than those of the executives of even the largest municipalities, there is little that the academic profession can do to remedy the situation in less than three or four decades. Nor, as far as I can see, can the professors do much more than complain (which they do automatically and with intense personal satisfaction in any case) about the regrettable lack of continuity in federal top-management. On the other hand the basic issue raised by the conference—the need for a trained administrative class in the civil service—is one that reaches to the very bedrock of social, governmental, administrative, and educational organization. If the universities can do little about the development of a corps of trained generalists on their own motion—since they do not control their market—it is equally true that nothing can be done unless the universities participate, either in bending the concept of administrative class preparation to academic notions of the content of a general education, as in Britain, or in accommodating themselves to the developing substance of the generalist function in a contemporary society, as is more likely to be the case in the United States. It is the purpose of this essay, therefore, to examine the possibility of the development of an administrative class "in harmony," as James Forrestal has phrased it, "with American traditions and fully recognizing the democratic spirit of American institutions."

All our confreres bemoaned the lack of experienced generalists in the public service. At times, in fact, the gathering, despite its dignity and erudition, seemed on the verge of breaking into a rollicking chorus of Ethel Waters' "A Good Man is Hard to Find!" They seemed also disposed to agree with Miss Waters that once found, a good man is expensive to keep. On the other hand, few of our colleagues bothered to define just what it is that they miss so poignantly. I retain the distinct impression that in some quarters mere ignorance of economics and law was regarded as *prima facie* evidence of qualification as a generalist. Donald Stone refers at several points in his essay to the characteristics of the top-management personnel—or the administrative class, as our British cousins prefer. Stone recognizes, in the first place, that there are variations even among the generalists, and that within the general context of the managerial concept there is a certain amount of specialization. He does, however, emphasize the importance of breadth, of knowledge reaching far beyond the policies, processes, and techniques of administration, into an understanding of the interplay of political, cultural, and social forces, of human nature and morale, and of the management of men with many and various types of skill and specialized knowledge. He underlines the importance of character—of the possession of a body of ideals and purposes "adequate to cope with current day forces toward social disintegration and friction in human relationships." James Forrestal speaks of the need for men with "breadth of experience, maturity of personality, and soundness of judgment . . . a capacity to deal with large matters of state . . . [and] who have the confidence of leading figures in both political parties." Pat French, without trying very hard, came reasonably close to an epigram: ". . . we can single out three kinds of people who were in scarce supply during the war and whose scarcity should be a matter of concern to those who are now planning higher education for the years ahead. These three are: people with perspective and insight into the nature of the governmental process; leaders without biases; and people who know how to run an organization." Speaking particularly of the problem of the foreign service George Kennan summed up as follows: ". . . it is a primary requirement for the successful foreign service officer that he be an emotionally robust individual: sensitive enough and thoughtful enough to avoid the bumptious obtuseness that sometimes goes with extroversion; yet not too deeply concentrated on himself and his own problems; imbued with an interest in and a liking for people, and a healthy curiosity for all that goes on about him, and capable of enjoying all the amenities of life in a foreign community without becoming beholden to any of them. For this we need men with a reasonable harmony of mental, physical, and emotional development, men with a strong sense of obligation and loyalty to whatever group they are associated with, and above all men with a sound American sense of humor, capable of recognizing and contemplating some of the sorry realities of the world in which we live without being plunged into overly tragic depths of gloom and despair."

Since no restrictions with respect to the admissibility of evidence were imposed upon the collaborators in this volume, I have taken the liberty of going afield from the conference essays themselves to search out a statement by one of our confreres which in my judgment is the best single package on the subject in the market. In his *Big Democracy* Paul Appleby writes as follows:

"The qualities include, perhaps first, an ability something like that required for higher mathematics. Trigonometry is no less practical and precise than arithmetic. It comprehends arithmetic, but is a way of relating and simplifying the handling of relationships between various arithmetical calculations. What is needed is the ability to handle relationships in their larger and broader terms—the quality of philosophy. This means a capacity to see public policy in tens of thousands of different actions and to relate these actions to each other in terms of public and governmental interest. Efficient 'operators' we have in great numbers. They are capable of serving well on the higher levels of governmental management only if they have this quality of philosophy.

"The kind of philosophy is of course important. A philosophy of absolutes and cold logic, a philosophy technical and rigid, would be ruinous. A sound political philosophy must comprehend people's spirits and emotions as well as their reasoned opinions; it must embody the logic of events and sentiments, and not merely the logic of statistics.

"The second quality needed by the top executive is 'governmental sense,' the ingrained disposition to put the public interest first and thus to recognize the great, essential and pervasive difference that distinguishes public administration from the management of private enterprise.

Rowland Egger

"Related to governmental sense is a third quality of public-relations or political sense. This involves, on the one hand, an appreciation of the necessity for governmental officials and governmental action to be exposed to the citizens and the public affected by them and, on the other, an ability to anticipate probable popular reaction and to make allowance for it. It also includes the capacity to act swiftly in introducing minor administrative adjustments when such action will relieve public irritation and the ability to sense major political shifts in the early stages of their development and gradually to modify the program of the agency accordingly. No matter how elevated they may be, however, administrators can never have the fullness of wisdom. Fortunately, they need not have it. Events and national sentiments will make the bigger and the ultimate decisions. Executives and administrative experts, working together, simply give form to specific programs and mechanisms within the framework of larger national movements. The capacity to sense the coming of these movements is political sense at its highest level.

"Ability to be governmental enough to discern the national interest and to insist on programs and procedures so sound that they will be as unyielding rock on which the waves of special interest may break their force in vain; ability to be political enough to seek those concessions which are the needed refinements of the process of making governmental action equitable and smooth; ability to be political enough to read and respond to the messages of public currents; and ability to use administrators who can organize and relate agencies so that they produce organized, integrated action—this is the combination of abilities required for the relatively few top people in the great agencies of government."

Significant as they are in suggesting the characteristics which ought in reasonable degree and in an infinite variety of combinations to be encountered among the managerial corps, there is obviously little in these word-pictures from which a job specification may be written or a civil service examination constructed. They do, on the other hand, convey a fairly definite notion of the nature of top-management operations. Thus skirting widely the semantic problem we may proceed to the exploration of measures which have been suggested for the development of an administrative class in the American public service.

The emphasis which has latterly come to be placed upon the civil servants of the generalist variety proceeds from two sources: (1) admiration for the truly notable achievements of the "elite corps" of the British civil service known as first division or administrative class employees, a group which numerically has never exceeded in normal times more than 1,500, which is less than 0.35 per cent of the prewar British civil service, and less than 2.5 per cent of the so-called "treasury" or general classes of the civil service; (2) a critical reappraisal of developments within the American bureaucracy which reveals important deficiencies with respect to continuity and consistent development in top management *expertise* and administrative policy.

In examining the applicability of British experience to the problems which have challenged the attention of the Bicentennial Conference, it is important to remember that the approach to recruitment, classification, and personnel management is strikingly similar in England and the United States for about 85 per cent of the civil service. In this group job specifications are just as detailed and precise, entrance standards just as specialized, and the whole process of fitting special skills to special jobs just as integral a part of personnel administration in London as in Washington. The remaining 15 per cent of the civil service employees are in the so-called "treasury" classes—a complete misnomer—and constitute a special corps. They fall into three main groups. The first division, or administrative class, consists of about 1,500 men, of whom some 450 are normally in training status, from which the permanent secretaries, deputy permanent secretaries, principal assistant secretaries, assistant secretaries, principals and assistant principals are drawn. The entrance examination requirements of the first division are geared closely to university curricula and to a considerable, though decreasing, extent this division constitutes the private hunting grounds of graduates of Oxford and Cambridge.

The second division, or executive class, is composed of about 5,000 employees responsible for "the higher work of supply and accounting departments and of other executive and specialized branches of the civil service. This . . . covers a wide field (including actuarial, legal, accounting, supply and statistical work) and requires in different degrees qualities of judgment, initiative, and resource. In the junior ranks it comprises the critical examination of particular cases of lesser importance not clearly within the scope of approved regulations or general decisions, initial investigations into matters of higher importance, and the immediate direction of small blocks of business. In its upper ranges it is concerned with matters of internal organization and control, with the settlement of broad questions arising out of business in hand or in contemplation, and with the responsible conduct of important operations."

The third division, or clerical class, numbers about 48,000. The generalized job description for this class includes "all the simpler clerical duties in the public departments, insofar as these are not assigned to Writing Assistants in accordance with the principles . . . (stated below) and in addition the following duties: dealing with particular cases in accordance with well-defined regulations, instructions or general practice; scrutinizing, checking and cross-checking straightforward accounts, claims, returns, etc., under well-defined instructions; preparation of material for returns, accounts and statistics in prescribed forms; simple drafting and *precis* work; collection of material on which judgments can be formed; supervision of the work of Writing Assistants." At the lower levels of the third division, the clerical assistant class (largely successor to the writing assistant class) is "employed on work preliminary to machine operations (punching, tabulating, etc.); on hand-copying and transcribing work (writing out acknowledgements, filling up forms, warrants, and bills); on the addressing of letters; on the counting and routine examination of postal orders, insurance cards, etc.; on the casting and preparation of schedules and lists, and the writing up of simple cards; and the custody of card indexes." In addition, shorthand typist and typist classes, performing the duties indicated in the titles and numbering some 7,500, complete the third division.

Finally, it is important to remember that as administrative institutions go the British civil service, and especially the administrative class, is a very modern development. In its present form this latter dates back only to 1920 when the treasury adopted most of the recommendations of a reorganization committee of the National Whitley Council. Its historical roots probably run back to an 1870 Order in Council which divided the clerical positions into two classes, accordingly as the work was "intellectual" or "routine." These institutional manifestations were, of course, eventually grounded in the recruitment theory embraced by the British public service around the middle of the last century, which emphasized the admission of young people into the service at prescribed ages, on the basis of open competitive examinations designed to indicate general ability and intelligence rather than technical proficiency or subject-matter specialization.

These points are labored thus lengthily because of the importance, to our consideration of the problem of developing an American administrative class, of the realization that with respect to 85 per cent of the civil service British and American approaches are for all practical purposes identical, and that with respect to the remaining 15 per cent there are many more points of similarity than of difference, while the fundamental incompatibilities to the degree that they exist turn on social

Rowland Egger

and political considerations rather than on administrative ones.

The problems and difficulties incident to the lack of an institutionalized administrative class in the American civil service were not discovered at Princeton. The deficiency has from time to time been remarked by scholars and commentators; de Tocqueville was the first, but by no means the last, to criticize systematically this defect in American administrative arrangements. More recently the Commission of Inquiry on Public Service Personnel made an exhaustive investigation of the problem. In many respects, the report of this commission in 1935 is comparable to the Macaulay report of 1854, for the clarity of its diagnosis and the simplicity and straightforwardness of its therapeutics. The findings of the Commission of Inquiry with respect to the need for an administrative class in the American civil service were strongly buttressed by the investigations of the President's Committee on Civil Service Improvement, headed by Justice Stanley Reed, which in 1941 emphatically reiterated the need for recognition of and institutionalization of recruitment for a generalist group in the federal service. And no knowledgeable person who reads Jerry Kluttz's daily column in *The Washington Post* (an unparalleled and entirely inadequately exploited source of administrative documentation, in my humble judgment) with any degree of fidelity can fail to realize that whatever the deficiencies of our institutional arrangements there exists already a very important nucleus for an administrative class in Washington.

It is, I think, pertinent at this point to look at the substance of the generalist function in modern government, apart from the previously discussed qualifications of the administrative officer. The Association of First Division Civil Servants submitted a statement to the British Royal Commission on the Civil Service in 1931 which summarizes the matter with great clarity from the British standpoint:

"The business of government, if it is to be well done, calls for the steady application of long and wide views to complex problems; for the pursuit, as regards each and every subject matter, of definite lines of action, mutually consistent, conformed to public opinion and capable of being followed continuously while conditions so permit and of being readily adjusted when they do not. Almost any administrative decision may be expected to have consequences which will endure or emerge long after the period of office of the Government by which or under whose authority it is taken. It is the special function of the civil service and the special duty of the administrative class of that service in their day-to-day work to set these wider and more enduring considerations against the exigencies of the moment, in order that the Parliamentary convenience of today may not become the Parliamentary embarrassment of tomorrow. . . . Vacillation, uncertainty, and inconsistency are conspicuous symptoms of bad administration. . . .

"Thus the efficient performance of the administrative work of the various departments calls in all cases for a trained mental equipment of high order, while in the particular case powers developed in some particular direction are needed. In some spheres what is most wanted is judgment, *savoir-faire*, insight and fair-mindedness; in others, an intellectual equipment capable of the ready mastery of complex and abstruse problems, for instance, taxation or other economic subjects; in others, imagination and constructive ability."

Writing against the distinctive background of the particularly American scene, the Commission of Inquiry on Public Service Personnel stated the problem in these clear and cogent terms in its 1935 report: "Under the American system of self-government, the voters elect legislative bodies and chief executives, and various other special officers, to make the laws, adopt the budgets, vote the taxes, and determine the general public policies. The actual doing of the work of government in accordance with these laws and policies is entrusted to appointed men and women. As it is impossible for the chief executive or for the legislative committees to deal with these men and women individually all the way down the line, each major activity is organized as a department, headed by an appointed or elected officer (called secretary, commissioner, or the like). The duties of this department head fall into two categories, political and administrative. Politically he is responsible to the chief executive or the electorate for carrying out in the work of his department the general political program of the dominant party. Administratively he is responsible for (a) interpreting the laws and regulations under which his department operates, (b) distributing the work of the department in such a way that the policies which have been determined may best be carried out, (c) maintaining consistency in the work of the department as between its various bureaus and activities and with other departments as well, (d) preserving continuity as between the past, the present, and the future of the work of the department, except of course where policy has been consciously altered, (e) keeping the department efficient and its personnel 'on its toes,' (f) reporting to the public, and being prepared to explain the work of the department. These latter duties are what the Commission means by administrative work. Since they are non-political, they could and should be assigned to career men in the administrative service. . . . In the federal government, we need only to recognize what has actually developed in certain departments at various times, and create in each department the definite position of Permanent Under Secretary and place this position in the career service. . . .

"The administrator is the link between the elective and appointive political service, on the one hand, and the professional and the clerical services on the other. He is differentiated from the political official, the 'executive' under our law, in that he does not make the important final decisions on political policy, does not advocate such policies before the electorate, and does not rise or fall on the basis of the acceptance or rejection of 'his' policies by the electorate or their elected representatives. These are the functions of the elected officials, who are therefore political and 'responsible.' The political officials serve as a buffer between the public and the administrators, interpreting public opinions and decisions and forcing them on the administration. If the elected official fails in his endeavors to lead the democratic procession, or at least to keep in front, he is dropped and another elected in his place.

"To the elected official the administrator is indispensable. The latter knows intimately the entire machine of government, is acquainted with its possibilities and limitations, and, through those who work with him, has command of the scores of technical and scientific facts and skills which must be correlated for the development and execution of any policy. And after a policy has been adopted, it is the administrator who translates the decision into reality through planning, organizing, and delegating, staffing, directing, coordinating and budgeting for the execution of the program within the limits assigned. In this process there are many important decisions of administrative policy to be made. These fall to the administrator to make, in harmony with the general program. If matters arise for which the general policy is no guide, or which may raise new or different political questions, these he must refer to the superior political official. Under a career administrative service, the administrator becomes extremely skillful in making the nice distinctions between political questions of policy and administrative questions of policy, because he rises in a service devoted to these matters.

"The relation of the administrator to the technical services is as follows. It is the administrator's responsibility to understand and coordinate public policy, and interpret it to the operating services. While he will have deep appreciation of and considerable intimate acquaintance with the operations of the technical and business departments, he cannot know their technology or science. No man can now be an expert in all fields. For the same reason, the technical and professional heads of these services can seldom if ever know the technologies or problems of their neighbors, or have a balanced view of the entire picture of government, or see what is necessary in their own work to produce in the end a correlated public service. In insisting on this correlation and conformity of work to the policies which have been adopted, the administrator is not interfering in technical work, which must of course be left to the technicians. He is, rather, applying to the technical field decisions of public policy, which, equally, are beyond the competence or responsibility of the technician."

The Reed Committee, after a careful look at the higher middle and top grades of the civil service, pointed out that the incumbents of these positions "perform the function of overhead management, direction and supervision in every branch of the Federal Government. This is the principal duty of bureau chiefs and assistant bureau chiefs, or directors of divisions and assistant directors, of heads of institutions, of the executive officers of commissions and their associates, and of a growing number of administrative assistants and assistants to executives in high positions. . . . In general terms, we think it would be helpful if the positions involving administrative duties were identified and carefully described in each department and agency, and if each department and agency made and kept current a list or inventory of persons who had demonstrated that they possessed administrative skill, with the personal and official history, present classification, and other relevant data. We also believe that the continuous search for good prospective material for administration should be more definitely recognized in some departments and agencies as a joint responsibility of supervisors and personnel officers. Finally, we think that the machinery is now for the first time available to permit a desirable extension of the program of training and testing which is already in operation in most departments.

In another place the Reed Committee called particular attention to the coordinative function which, as British experi-

An Administrative Class?

ence has clearly demonstrated, is enormously facilitated by the existence of a homogeneous administrative class: "Government departments and agencies, their divisions and their subdivisions, suffer from an insularity which hampers their effective coordination as parts of a single whole. Indifference, jealousy, competition, and sometimes even sabotage develop in the effort of each small unit to protect itself and its staff. There is too little recognition of a common responsibility to a common and single employer, the American people as represented by the Congress and the President."

It would, however, be misleading to infer that among the commentators and investigators there is anything like agreement or unanimity with respect to the practicability of establishing an administrative class in the American civil service. Lewis Meriam, in his *Public Personnel Problems*, raises a number of objections to the notion of the administrative class. He suggests that the federal system in the United States has resulted in the allocation of general staff functions to the national authorities in many segments of governmental activity, while operations remain at the state level and subject to state policy within broad limits. The functions of the federal official tend to be the collection of facts and statistics, research, investigation, propaganda, promotion, and largely advisory supervision. These, he thinks, are not the functions of an administrative class official, and he points to the inadequate development of the research and investigatory function in British administration as evidence of the failure of the administrative class in this area. He is likewise of the opinion that at this late date we will never in the United States be able to superimpose an "administrative class" on the professional, technical, and scientific employees, because our reaction from the spoils system has exalted the professional and scientific group at the expense of the "administrative" group formerly composed mainly of spoils appointees. Moreover, if the services traditionally administered by scientists-turned-executive are excluded, there would be, he says, only about 1,000 administrative class positions in the entire federal service, which means that the number of new appointments per annum necessary to maintain it would be infinitesimal—or anyway too small to interest American universities.

Moreover, Lewis Meriam questions bluntly the assumption that administrative ability is inconsistent with professional competence. Staff agencies of the research, investigational, and promotional type, he points out, are small and present few large problems of general organization and management. On the other hand, they do require a large measure of professional competence and standing. He goes on to name a group of officials in which professional competence is implicit in their titles —the Surgeon General of the Public Health Service, the Commissioner of Education, the Director of the Bureau of Agricultural Economics, the Director of the Bureau of Standards, the Director of the Geological Survey, etc. He continues: "Proponents of a special administrative class sometimes contend that scientific and technical men lack administrative ability. . . . Ability to cite some cases in which scientific and technical men lack administrative ability does not prove that all scientific and technical men lack administrative ability, any more than ability to cite some cases in which scientific and technical men were outstanding administrators proves that all such men are excellent administrators. No evidence has yet been adduced to prove that in America, under our educational system, a general academic education produces better administrators than a more vocational education, or that graduates of general arts who do not go on into professional fields are superior in administrative ability to graduates in arts who subsequently get professional education. In the absence of sound statistics one must resort to observation. Observation suggests that administrative ability and interest are something rather separate and distinct from fields of learning and that good administrators and poor administrators may be found in almost any field."

An Administrative Class?

Meriam makes a good deal of the psychological handicaps of junior administrators, inducted as heirs apparent to administrative empires, and of the difficulties which a favored position throws in the way of securing cooperation and effectively leading an organization. He sums up his position on this point as follows: "The English system works because the members of the administrative division constitute a caste which occupies all the positions from top to bottom within that division. It is highly questionable whether it would work if it were not a caste and if there were real competition among two or more divisions for upper positions. If the caste ever loses full and complete control of the upper positions, its own days are probably numbered."

Differences in recruitment theory and policy, the broadening of technical and professional education and of civil service examinations for technical and professional positions, and the alleged inapplicability in Great Britain of the "administrator" principle to smaller agencies and smaller governments are also cited, but his main indictment of the administrative class proposal rests upon the grounds which have been outlined.

The essentials of the British approach to administrative class education and recruitment have been thoroughly covered in Sir James Grigg's essay, and need not be labored here. Professor Woodward sums it up by saying that "one of the most remarkable achievements of the English in the nineteenth century was to devise a mode of education which gave to the English upper middle class the qualities of an old governing aristocracy." Nor was he hesitant to urge strongly the case for classical learning—instruction in Latin and Greek—as an important base for the type of education required by an administrator, although he recognizes, albeit with a certain reluctance, the trends in English education which are tending to place increased emphasis upon "newer" subjects such as economics, public administration, and the history and working of institutions, the educational value of which in his opinion is by no means well established. While Sir James Grigg skillfully avoided commitment with respect to the appropriate subject matter for an administrative class education—beyond observing that if he had it to do over again he would not submit the unholy alliance of mathematics and natural science—he is completely unequivocal in his support of subject-matter irrelevancy in administrative class preparation.

The completely charming essays of Professor Woodward and Sir James Grigg actually demonstrate most of all how profoundly educational traditions can diverge within a general *milieu* of cultural similarity, and how drastically different social and administrative patterns may become under the aegis of a common legal system. Even those who have been privileged to participate at first hand in the absorbing educational processes of an English university cannot but realize that the game is being played under a set of rules all but incomprehensible to outsiders—and whether the rules are for Lilliputians or Brobdingnagians only time can tell.

On the whole, I am inclined to the view that American experience tends to sustain Lewis Meriam's view that administrative ability and interest are something rather separate and distinct from fields of learning. For my own part, and speaking as one subjected to the rigors of an exceptionally drastic classical education, I can affirm that more often than not in America, and occasionally at Oxford itself, Aristophanes and Aeschylus are taught by mere linguistic grease-monkeys, and their educational and cultural content is somewhat below that of a good course in horseshoeing. On the other hand, and I apologize again for a personal reference, the university course which affected me most profoundly and opened up vistas of humanistic knowledge which I had completely overlooked before was a lecture series in the School of Engineering dealing with the history of sewage disposal in ancient and medieval times. Here it was that Catullus, Livy, Tacitus, Horace, Petronius, Juvenal,

An Administrative Class?

Plautus, and Terence came to life—here the real significance of Roman engineering and legal genius became apparent—and here the elementary connection between the development of urban civilization (which is to say the development of civilization) and the growth of man's ingenuity in disposing of animal waste became clear and I began to understand and appreciate its decisive influence in the cultural development of modern man.

Moreover, and with no more than a fleeting regret for the terrific waste which this confesses, it may be observed that there is very little Aristotle ever wrote that Jowett did not improve substantially in the translating.

The Meriam postulate that administrative ability and interest are apart and distinct from subject matter fields implies that the art of managing men probably cannot be taught through formal instructional mechanisms. Sir James Grigg would, of course, agree with this position. From this point, however, the argument diverges sharply. Since the art of managing men cannot be taught, Sir James and Professor Woodward proceed to the position that only a cultural education (phrase of argument-begging import) imparting a sense of form and facile perception of relativities constitutes a proper administrative class education. The Commission of Inquiry and the Reed Committee would respond that even if the art of managing men cannot be imparted by formal instructional methods, the principles and practices involved in the scientific use of the tools of management can be taught. Lewis Meriam would insist that between the politicians on the one hand and the professional and technical staff on the other there is no place for an administrative class, and no need for one even if a place could be found, so why bother trying to educate one.

Let us take the evidence, before closing this phase of the argument, of one of the professional scientists whose ghosts Lewis Meriam invokes so freely and casually. Dr. W. W. Stockburger, one of the great career officials of the federal service, started out as an instructor in botany at Denison University, later became physiologist in charge of drug and related plants in the Bureau of Plant Industry, and eventually wound up as director of personnel of the United States Department of Agriculture. Out of his long, rich, and varied experience as scientist and as administrator Dr. Stockburger writes as follows: "Specialized training in the law or the sciences is an inadequate foundation upon which to build an administrative career. . . . Administration, although not separate and apart from the activity administered, involves a series of relationships not inherent in what is to be administered, but superimposed upon it. The understanding of the nature of these relationships and of the art of utilizing them effectively will be facilitated by a mastery of the principles of public administration and an exploration of the content of the social sciences. If government is to secure for the public service recruits who have the capacity to become satisfactory administrators, our educational institutions must be induced to afford selected students an opportunity to acquire a perspective of the relations of governmental operations to the public interest much broader than that usually developed in the standardized technical courses."

The evidence is easier to recite than to apply. Stockburger the plant physiologist, which is the dominant *motif* of his career, is to a considerable degree the proof of Lewis Meriam's assertion that technical and administrative ability are not incompatible and are frequently encountered in the same person. But Stockburger the humanist and student of administration, a facet only imperceptibly inferior to his scientific side, would be the first to deny Meriam's conclusions with respect to administrative class education and is, in fact, our most positive witness and ardent advocate in behalf of the systematic preparation of administrative personnel.

Of all the proposals which have been made for the establishment of an administrative career service in the United States government, that of the Commission of Inquiry on Public Service Personnel is at once the most comprehensive, the best documented, and the most knowledgeable with regard to the immediate and long-run implications of the undertaking. The pertinent portions of the commission's report merit our careful attention at this point.

The Commission of Inquiry proposed that the public service be organized in five major groups or divisions: (1) the administrative group, comprehending the personnel involved in general management, including organizing, staffing, directing, coordinating, planning, budgeting, and reporting; (2) the professional group, including those who use the special techniques and knowledge mastered by the recognized professions, such as medicine, engineering, law, architecture, chemistry, social work, and teaching; (3) the clerical group, covering those who perform the office work of handling the business and papers and records and reports which every large scale enterprise must maintain; (4) the skilled and trades group, including carpenters, plumbers, masons, steel workers, mechanics, electricians, painters, printers, etc.; (5) the unskilled group, covering ordinary day labor.

These five groups, the commission felt, constituted the basis for reasonably self-contained, though by no means air-tight, separate career services, within which entrants would climb their appropriate career ladders and work out their proper destinies. The commission emphasized certain specific conditions which must be met in order to establish and maintain any of the proposed career services. "There must be public acceptance, acknowledgment and general understanding of the career services, and an appreciation on the part of professional and scientific groups, the learned societies and the press of the distinctions between the services and the nature of the contributions of each to the total work of government." For each of the five services the commission proposed that there should be "an appropriate method of entrance based solely on the character-

Rowland Egger

istics and capacities of the applicant, and so defined that the conditions of entrance would be relatively stable and easily understood." The commission points out that "inasmuch as a 'career' presupposes a lifetime of work of growing knowledge and skill, entrance should be limited, in the ordinary course of events, to the lowest positions within each service and to a young group of entrants. A career cannot be said to exist if top positions are generally recruited from outside, from men who do not understand the work, and in such a way as to create an effective bar to advancement from the bottom to the top of the service itself." It particularly emphasizes that "opportunity for advancement and promotion within each career service must be open to all within the service on the basis of work alone and capacity for the higher post. Each service must be viewed in the broadest possible light so that the top posts may be filled from a wide base and so that those who enter at the bottom may have the opportunity of reaching great eminence." The commission draws particular attention to its view that "wherever careers in the public service are virtually identical with careers in private life, the definition of the service, the system of training, the method of entrance, the opportunities for advancement, and the compensation should be definitely related, and opportunities for transfer back and forth should be provided. But where the nature of the public work is clearly unique, or governed by different or conflicting motives, the method of recruitment and the conditions of service should be different, and transfers back and forth should be scrutinized with care." The establishment of professional, scientific, and other associations within the service, as well as organizations for considering conditions of service and for ministering to the social life of the group is strongly encouraged by the commission.

Obviously, the recruitment policies embraced condition more than any other single factor the outworking of the program. The commission is quite fearless in "laying it on the line" in this respect as well. It suggests:

An Administrative Class?

(1) The unskilled group would be "recruited without reference to education, on the basis of fitness for the work, determined entirely by practical tests, usually on the job. While most men would enter the service after grade school, or perhaps after two years of high school, there would be no particular age limit."

(2) The skilled and trades group would be recruited "after education, which normally would not extend beyond high school, on the basis of the mastery of particular skills and trades. Admission should be competitive through practical tests, with entrance age limits so computed as to bring the examination soon after the completion of apprenticeship."

(3) The clerical group is divided into two sub-groups, the strictly clerical and the clerical-executive divisions. The clerical group "would be recruited after not less than two years of high school and be trained for the special techniques of their jobs after entry. Age limits would thus be set at possibly sixteen to seventeen, and the examination would deal primarily with general intelligence and with the subjects these young men and women have been taking in school. . . . The clerical-executive group would be taken at a later stage, that is, after general high school education. The age limit should be set at eighteen to nineteen, and the examination should be related to high school subjects. If special training in business colleges is required, it should be given after selection."

(4) The professional group would be "recruited after special training, but before practical experience. The appropriate age limits are from twenty-three to twenty-eight, and the examinations should deal almost exclusively with the mastery of the special training. An extremely useful device in the recruitment of professional service is the requirement that the candidate shall possess the certificate of the appropriate accredited professional or scientific bodies or associations."

(5) The administrative group would be selected from "those with an advanced general education immediately upon the

completion of that education. The appropriate examination is one which will seek to determine which of the young men and women who present themselves during a given year have at that stage of development attained an outstanding position among their fellows of the same age group in the pursuit of general knowledge. The examination should determine primarily what the candidates are, not what they know about the work for which they are to be trained in the future."

The commission reiterates at a number of points in the course of its report that it is not proposing a closed career service. There will be times, it believes, when it may be necessary to bring from outside the particular career service persons with extensive practical experience into advanced posts which require such practical experience; there is no abrogation of the career principle, the commission says, provided the normal course of promotion is retained on a career basis. Moreover, the commission views the system which it proposes as providing not a series of pigeonholes on an organization chart, but rather a series of ladders, starting at different ages and after different periods of education and experience, and arriving eventually at different points. The commission believes it to be a matter of prime importance that the ladders should not be so far apart that the unusual employee will be unable to pass from one ladder to another on the basis of additional education or experience.

The chapter dealing with administrative and management personnel in the report of the President's Committee on Civil Service Improvement, submitted in 1941, was undoubtedly the high point of the committee's work. Unfortunately, it had fallen so "flat on its face" in the teapot tempest over the status of lawyers in the federal service that it never thereafter really recovered its dignity or self-confidence, so that even at its boldest it is a little less than incisive. Gordon Clapp has summed up with both clarity and charity the committee's proposals in the following words: "The Committee's recommendations visualize the creation of an administrative group with or without professional or scientific specializations consisting of incumbents having administrative responsibilities in positions occupying grades CAF-11, P-4, and higher. This administrative career service corps would be replenished largely by promotion or transfer from within the service with primary reliance as to method of selection placed in the hands of examining committees and the discriminating judgments of superior administrative officers and departmental personnel officers. Furthermore, the Committee urges recognition of the role of general management in the career service directly below the policy-making heads, the general managers constituting the top rank of the administrative corps. It is significant to note that the Committee does not participate directly in the time-worn controversy as to whether persons for administrative responsibility should be drawn from among those of professional or technical training and experience or from among those whose training and experience are devoid of such specialization. The Committee wisely accepts the fact that higher administrative positions are and will be occupied by persons from both backgrounds. They rightly identify the higher administrative group upon the basis of the common denominator of administrative skill and responsibility."

The committee, in choosing to avoid the difficult political and social problems inherent in the establishment of an administrative class through the creation of a definite selection procedure and the provision of a definite career ladder leading to the top management positions, ignored the central problem of how to secure subordinate personnel competent to assume the management responsibilities of the upper echelons. The administrative capacities of the people in CAF-11, P-4, and higher exercising administrative responsibility will be no better than the potential administrative capacity recruited at the entrance levels. In and of themselves, the committee's recommendations do nothing to improve the administrative potentialities of the input at the bottom. It is not denied, of course, that the recognition of a managerial corps in the civil service which the committee proposes would have a salutary effect. But this recognition is not the heart of the matter, and I am not reassured even by Clapp's subsequent reference to the mitigating effects of "existing mysteries of human potentiality" in overcoming inadequate selection procedures.

The events which have transpired in the twelve years since the Commission of Inquiry on Public Service Personnel reported have served in large measure to validate and reemphasize the recommendations then made. Despite a very considerable expansion in the numbers of employees with general administrative abilities produced by the successive federal relief and public works programs, including the inauguration of the social security program, the war found us with an alarming deficiency in the administrative group. During the war an enormous administrative machine was hastily put together, composed mainly of recruits from business and the professoriate, built in many cases around general administrators who themselves had barely had time to get their rough edges smoothed off in the relief, works, and social security programs. Since the war all of the businessmen, most of the professors, and a goodly number of the trained administrators have left. It will be an interesting, but probably not very edifying, spectacle to watch the organization of ERP, and we may be virtually assured that a new group of appointees will recapitulate *in toto* every mistake that was ever made from FERA to the present, in addition to inventing a large number of new and unique errors. This is one of the minor costs of not having an administrative class with a well-established and generally accepted role in federal top management.

The proposals of the commission, it should be noted, involve no de-emphasis of professional education and training, which is a special characteristic of American education. Nor is the administrative service ladder closed to those who start off their careers in professional and technical fields. There is no reason to think that a career system such as the commission contemplates would not produce its W. W. Stockburgers, its William Alanson Whites, and its Ellen C. Potters, or that any of them would encounter difficulty in switching over from the professional to the administrative ladder, and perhaps back again, as the occasion required. On the other hand, the commission's proposals would assure a reservoir of generally educated employees in junior administrative positions throughout the service from which the higher administrative echelons would normally be renewed. After all, most M.D.'s had rather practice medicine than hold the moist hands of nervous politicians.

The objection to the establishment of an administrative class based upon social grounds—the creation of a privileged class of bright young college graduates in the government—never actually had much foundation, and at the present time, when a college education is literally within reach of everyone who desires one, is a factor of no consequence whatever. Moreover, as the lack of continuity in federal topside management clearly indicates, the democratic ideal is not applied in the public service today to the extent that uncritical opinion supposes. As Harold Dodds pointed out a decade ago: "There exists a practical deadline in our national and local governments between, say, the position of chief clerk and the position of directing head of a bureau or agency. Unfortunately, however, it is politics that too often enforces the deadline. The highest posts are rarely filled by promotions within the service. . . . The proposal here made looks to equipping the service so that it will be able to supply within itself executives of the highest type. . . . As long as the top ranks are open only to outsiders, whether to politicians, or to lawyers, college professors and successful businessmen called in for brief periods from the outside, public administration as a career will enjoy low prestige and will fail to attract its fair share of the best ability in the country."

Rowland Egger

I conclude, therefore, that there is nothing worthy of the attention of the Thomas committee in the proposal to create an administrative class in the American public service, and that the establishment of such an institution is wholly compatible with the spirit and traditions of an egalitarian society. As the Commission of Inquiry foresaw, and the Bicentennial Conference reaffirmed, it must necessarily be an institution which will reflect the special characteristics of American culture. It cannot be permitted to become the private property either of the Ivy League or the several centers of higher education which purport to teach all the mysteries of the administrative inner sanctum. It will also have to make provision for the "rare bird" who is too busy getting an education to go to college. And while its prime objective is the production, recruitment, and training of generalists, it will be compelled to avoid the rigidity which would exclude from the administrative career service qualified persons whose only disability is that in the misguided enthusiasm of their youth they acquired a professional degree.

The limitations of an American career administrative service ought also to be recognized. It should not be expected to accomplish some things that the British administrative class, with its old-school-tie social coherence, has done. It cannot bear the burden of responsibility in its corporate capacity for interdepartmental and interagency coordination of program and operations in anything like the degree to which the British service is called upon to exercise this function. Although the British service is not without its institutional facilities, both in the Treasury and in the entourage of the Prime Minister, for coordination, the degree of reliance upon institutional facilities will inevitably be much greater in the United States. Moreover, administrative class officials in the United States probably will never exercise the broad degree of control over administrative operations common to the British service, if for no other reason than that the Secretary will generally be under foot, whereas his British counterpart is normally out of the way down at the House of Commons, or back home buttering up his constituency. Finally, it will be at least fifteen or twenty years after an administrative career service is established before its significant results begin to become apparent.

As a concluding observation, I should like to suggest that the establishment of an administrative career service would have a terrifically sobering effect upon instruction in American universities. For many years we have experimented gaily and irresponsibly in devising courses and reshuffling course combinations, improvising in course content and method, and generally using students for the guinea pigs many of them turn out to be. The erection of definite objective standards of comparison will inevitably affect profoundly our attitudes toward both content and teaching methods. Such a change, by and large, could not come too soon.

15

MANAGING THE PUBLIC'S BUSINESS

BY JAMES FORRESTAL

In its broadest sense public service is the business of all of us. Practically everyone gainfully employed is serving the public; the engineer, the garage owner, the teacher, the worker on the farm and in the factory, the salesman of either goods or services, the doctor, the lawyer, heads of corporations, senators and congressmen—all are engaged in public service and they build the foundations upon which government rests. For the present purpose, however, we may look at the subject in the more limited terms of service to the executive branches of the federal government.

It may be well to remark very briefly about government itself. The business of government is truly a matter of we, the people. There is no such abstraction as a mythical "they" upon whom we can unload complaints and criticisms. I have heard "they" frequently used when it is desired to allocate responsibility for troubles or mistakes. But I have never seen in business, in the federal service bureaucracy, or in the military services any group of men who could be identified as the single group source of power and responsibility. In our government that is not possible; our government decisions are composite decisions and no one man or small group of men can make them.

In totalitarian governments the "they" concept may be accurate, i.e. the concept of a small number of men acting upon what they conceive to be a permanent mandate of the people to manage their affairs. In countries like the United States and Great Britain and other truly democratic societies, however, such mandates from the people are intermittent and come up periodically for a renewal of their validity. That is what the political scientists call the principle of legitimacy—that government power flows from the people upward, not from the masters downward.

It has frequently been remarked that, in those modern states which undertake to retain democratic institutions and principles of representative and republican government, it is necessary to maintain the difficult relationship between those persons holding office as a result of the expression of the political will of the people and the career administrators who are necessary for the orderly operation of governmental machinery.

The politician, and I use that in the best sense of the word to mean the man who holds elective office, is apt to deal with public affairs on an expedient basis, reflecting the shifting tides of public opinion. I do not criticize him for that. He is the channel by which the people communicate their wishes and sometimes, if you will, their prejudices. He has to be conscious that a leader, if he is to remain one, needs to be sure of a following. When Lord John Russell said, "I am a leader, therefore I must follow them" he stated a political truism which is not necessarily a confession of weakness.

We can never get away from the advice that the Honorable Sam Rayburn, then Speaker of the House, first gave me when I came to Washington—that if you want to be a statesman you first have to get elected.

The genius and the tradition of our government demand the constant meshing of the will of the people with sound administration. Sir William Harcourt said: "Political heads of departments are necessary to tell the civil service what the public will not stand." The administrative expert, in other words, is an invaluable servant but an impossible master.

The American government has gone through a history of accommodation between these two conflicting forces—the political instinct for quick response to the people's wishes and the principles of sound administration which sometimes irk the people whom it is proposed to serve. The early Federalists built their ideas of government upon the concept of the Greek republics that the educated, the trained, and the more responsible should be the masters of affairs. Under Andrew Jackson this concept was destroyed and scrapped in favor of greater participation by the average citizen, with the result that the phrase, "To the victors belong the spoils" had special application to the federal government. For fifty years this remained the method of federal administration, and every four years, broadly speaking, there was a complete overturn of personnel in Washington.

Then in 1883 the civil service in the United States government was born and was given a substantial impetus by a great practical political leader—Grover Cleveland. The Civil Service Commission has made great strides in improving the competence and efficiency of personnel, by furthering job classifications and the equitable distribution of promotion and increase of pay. However, it has never been given the responsibility for providing top management talent.

From the recent writings and discussions of those concerned with government personnel, there have emerged certain conclusions upon which there seems to be broad agreement: One of these is that there is a great need for, and a present lack of, top management executive personnel in our federal government; second, that there is a need for continuity of direction in the executive branch of government; and finally, that there is a need for the leavening influence of practical and human experience and judgment on the specialized skills and vocabularies of the professional government servant.

A number of writers have dealt with the lack of continuity in administrative personnel of federal departments and offices. I can speak with some conviction to that point because when I came to the Department of the Navy with Frank Knox in the summer of 1940 there was no high-ranking civilian official to whom we could turn for administrative advice. Yet we were immediately charged with the responsibility for the administration of vastly increased appropriations (in the five years of the procurement program of 1940 to 1945, navy expenditures totaled over 90 billions).

I submit that our experience is sufficient evidence of the need of a permanent under-secretary or assistant secretary who can provide the politically appointed department head with a background of knowledge so that when it is called upon to face substantial expansion there is at least a small cadre of trained people to provide the advice and guidance which any newcomer to government will need. Such a cadre of trained civilians is as necessary in my judgment as the trained naval officers themselves on the military side, if we are to meet demands of sudden and sharp expansion for war.

In the British government this continuity is provided by a small group of executive and administrative personnel in the British civil service. One of the contributors to this volume, Sir James Grigg, formerly Secretary of State for War in the British Cabinet and recently representing Great Britain in the affairs of the International Bank for Reconstruction, has given us an account of the workings of the British civil service. His remarks and those of other observers make it clear that there are fundamental differences in the governmental methods of the two countries.

The British Cabinet is the creature of the House of Commons; it is the maker of policy for the party in power and it speaks with the full authority of that party and therefore with the authority of the House. Political appointees in the British Cabinet head their various departments but the continuity of professional administrative skill is provided by permanent under-secretaries in each of the great departments of state.

Our Constitution and our habits of government do not permit an exactly similar system because with us Cabinet members do not sit in either house of Congress; they are the appointees of the President and they are always open to the charge that they have received no mandate of popular election.

Several observers, in particular Mr. Patterson H. French, now Assistant to the Director of the Bureau of the Budget, have referred to the difficulty, during the late war, in filling top management positions. Three kinds of people, he remarked, were in scarce supply: people with perspective and insight into the nature of the governmental processes; leaders without bias; and people who know how to run an organization. He pointed out that government by its very nature is essentially a big enterprise and that the mere size of government requires more than the ordinary capacity for clear, definite assignment of duties, for creating a system without at the same time creating red tape and above all, for that *sine qua non* of the administrator, the ability to reduce human frictions to a minimum.

These needs add up to what I have felt for a long time to be a major need of government—the training of the people competent to exercise responsibility at the top levels of government management.

There is, of course, one danger common to all government activities. That is the danger of corrosion, of inertia, and of regarding jobs as sinecures rather than as a means of constructive and useful service to the people. Anyone who has ever had anything to do with any large organization is thoroughly aware that this is one of the great difficulties of management, the weeding out of the misfits and the mediocre. The military services have only partially solved this problem and any business executive who is entirely honest will admit that business has never completely solved it. It is one of the greatest dangers in the creation of a professional class of government administrators. It can only be met by high standards of selection and some means by which those who do not show adequate promise of future development may be screened out of the service.

Managing the Public's Business

Among informed observers, there is general agreement that complete reliance cannot be placed upon technical skills and that common sense and other basic human virtues must remain the essence of democratic governmental practice. For many reasons this strikes a particularly sympathetic chord. I recall the distinguished governor of New York State, the late Alfred E. Smith, who combined in himself so much of the practical in both politics and economics, who was not a scholar but was aware of the uses of scholarship. Like many other great men, Smith was almost universal in his genius. Not only was he a master of the political process and of the administrative areas of government, but he was also a sociologist, a practical economist and, above all, a human being. He was truly a child of the sidewalks of New York and he was always one of the common people. The combination of native character and honesty, and of his practical education in a professional political organization, gave him a genuine rather than a synthetic appreciation of the problems of people. In the board of aldermen in the city of New York and then in the assembly of the state legislature he formed a pragmatic governmental philosophy and a capacity for orderly thinking unsurpassed by any American.

I doubt if Al Smith ever took any courses in government as such, nor was he a lawyer. Yet his knowledge of the basic law of New York State was so profound that to him Elihu Root gave the major credit for the great work of rewriting the Constitution of New York State in 1915. And when he lectured before a group of the Harvard faculty in January of 1929, he gave extemporaneously so masterful a presentation of the remaining weaknesses of the government of the State of New York that Felix Frankfurter observed that if Harvard had good sense it would make him a professor of law at that university the next morning.

The other side of the medal, however, is this: There are not many Al Smiths and we cannot depend upon such political accidents to provide for the great tasks of administration in the federal government. In the first place there is no guaranty that the Al Smiths will get elected and in the second place it is doubtful if even such a political and administrative genius as Governor Smith himself could run the federal government today without a corps of competent administrators and executives.

There has been general agreement that the increasing complexity of the social and economic problems within our country and the equally great complexity and delicacy of external relationships force us to search for men who will make a career of government and to whom government can offer opportunities at the highest levels of administrative and executive responsibility. The almost fearful foreshortening of space and telescoping of time compel different procedures from those required in the times of Washington, Jackson, and Woodrow Wilson.

The central theme of this book is university education in its relation to public service. I think it is appropriate, therefore, to inquire what kind of education will best prepare men for government work and as a corollary what the universities can do to improve citizen responsibility.

The French and the Germans have relied largely upon specialized education in the training of their public servants.

The British have relied upon broad cultural and scientific training, designed to give men power of independent thought, ability for clear and lucid expression of ideas and, possibly the most important of all, what may be called the humanistic attitude that government shall remain the servant, and not become the master, of the people.

I believe the broad general training is preferable. Without wishing to step on the toes of any of my associates in Washington, where toe-stepping can be a very dangerous business indeed, I have observed what seems to me to be some imbalance in the predominance of statisticians, lawyers, and economists in our government as contrasted to the number of men drawn from a more general experience. Training in the categories I have named is useful, but I suggest that sometimes people with such specialized training tend to rely too much on the techniques of their training to the detriment of practical solutions.

What is good administration? There is no firm definition. From my own experience it seems to me that it is largely a capacity for identifying areas which need broad policy direction, then seeing that a workable policy is formed and, finally, following up with the dustpan of good execution to see that the policy decisions are carried out.

To sum up, it seems to me that these general conclusions can be drawn: The federal government will require in the years ahead of us the services of men with broad foundations of liberal education and, if possible, with some exposure to the practical matters of business and politics, who will make government service a professional career. To these men should be open the post of under-secretary or of assistant secretary in all of the departments of the federal government so that those departments may have a continuity of administrative knowledge as a supplement to the political judgment and skill of the cabinet member or political appointee who heads the department or office.

In order to attract young men of ability to such a career, rewards must be increased by lifting the present salary ceilings, by providing some better form of security when the peak of their working lives is passed and, possibly most important of all, by providing some additional attraction in terms of increased prestige.

The Congress of the United States has recently made substantial changes in its own administrative procedures which would fit in with my proposal—changes which involved consolidation of committees and an increase in the staff facilities available to members. A parallel streamlining is indicated in the executive branches. The precise form which it should take is, of course, a matter for the Congress—the methods of initial selection, and equally important, the method of separation; the situs of administration and supervision whether in the Bureau of the Budget or the Treasury Department or the Civil Service Commission; the means by which the universities could best contribute to such a program.

A first step has been taken in the appointment of a bipartisan commission to study the need for improved administration and the proposals advanced for filling the needs. I do not want to oversimplify the problem but I believe an excellent start could be made by making early statutory provision for a permanent under-secretary or an assistant secretary in all of the departments, as well as providing a proper basis for their selection.

The adoption of such a proposal by Congress would impose on our universities the major responsibility for training the required public servants as well as the ordinary citizen students. To those who propose to enter the service of government the university training should have as its objectives the capacity for clear thinking, for lucidity and clarity of expression and, above all, for the application of understanding and pragmatic methods, rather than dogmatic methods, to the human problems which are and always will be the main problems of government.

For the rest of its student body university education should be directed to the end that the young men leaving college should have a sense of responsibility beyond the immediate one of earning a living. They have been, so to speak, endowed by society, and they must make some return for that investment. "Princeton in the nation's service" was the phrase used so often and so aptly by Woodrow Wilson. If our country is to continue to prove the workability of democratic institutions that phrase must be a living reality and not merely a slogan. The aim of education must also include the humility which is the foundation of sound scholarship; it must emphasize that it is the use of education and not the education itself which matters. As I said earlier, Al Smith was not a scholar but he was fully aware of the advantages of scholarship. He made ample use of its methods because he had learned on the hard and practical road of experience what others had obtained from formal education.

Another field in which the university can contribute to the public service is in that of adult education. Some initial steps have already been taken. I hope that others will follow; in doing so it is of the highest importance that such education be objective and scholarly in the highest sense, that it be free of propaganda, and that it conform to the basic principles of the kind of democratic society that this country represents.

The universities of this country, both the state and the privately endowed, have already made a great contribution to the public service. The American universities and the public service are and should be practically synonymous. Universities exist essentially for that service.

In the narrower sense of public service our universities served on a far broader scale during the late war than ever before. To the army and navy it was a service that was indispensable. In the years of peace we in government expect to maintain close contacts with our universities through as many avenues as possible. The benefits will be mutual and not the least among them will be the opportunity to convince our young men and women that public service is the foundation of citizenship and the only real insurance for a continuation of our free society.

WHO'S WHO OF CONTRIBUTORS

PAUL H. APPLEBY. Formerly a newspaper and radio executive. Served as Under Secretary of Agriculture (1940-1944) and as Assistant Director of the U.S. Bureau of the Budget. Author of *Big Democracy*. Now Dean of the Maxwell School of Citizenship and Public Affairs, Syracuse University.

SELDEN CHAPIN. Appointed to the Foreign Service in 1925; has held various positions including Director of the Office of Foreign Service. Now serving as Minister to Bulgaria.

FREDERICK S. DUNN. Author of *The Practice and Procedure of International Conferences, The Protection of Nationals*, and other works. Formerly with Johns Hopkins University. Now, Director, Yale Institute of International Studies.

ROWLAND A. EGGER. Former Director of the Budget, Virginia (1939-1942); formerly general manager and director of the Corporación Bolivana de Fomento (1942-1945). Now on faculties of the University of Virginia and Columbia University.

ARTHUR S. FLEMMING. Formerly Director of the School of Public Affairs, American University (1934-1939). Served with the Office of Production Management and as a member of the War Manpower Commission. Served as a U.S. Civil Service Commissioner from 1939 to 1948. Now, President of Ohio Wesleyan University.

JAMES FORRESTAL. Investment banker; President of Dillon, Read & Co. (1937-1940). Under Secretary of the Navy (1940-1944); Secretary of the Navy (1944-1947). Secretary of Defense (1947—).

PATTERSON H. FRENCH. Formerly on faculties of Williams, Union, and Yale. Former staff member, Committee on Public Administration, Social Science Research Council.

Served with Office of Price Administration. Now, Assistant to the Director, U.S. Bureau of the Budget.

JOHN M. GAUS. Author of *Reflections on Public Administration, Public Administration and the U.S. Department of Agriculture,* and other works. Formerly on the faculty of the University of Wisconsin; now Professor of Government at Harvard University.

SIR (PERCY) JAMES GRIGG, K.C.B., K.C.S.I. Entered the Civil Service in 1913; served as Permanent Under Secretary of State for War, 1939-1942, and as Secretary of State for War, 1942-1945; later, British Executive Director of the International Bank for Reconstruction and Development.

H. STRUVE HENSEL. Served as chief of procurement, legal division, as general counsel, and as Assistant Secretary of the Navy during World War II. Now with Carter, Ledyard and Milburn, New York City.

GEORGE F. KENNAN. A foreign service officer since his graduation from Princeton (1925). Counselor to the American delegation, European Advisory Commission (1944); Minister-Counselor, Moscow (1945). Later, Deputy for Foreign Affairs, National War College. Now, Director, Policy Planning Staff, State Department.

ROBERT A. LOVETT. Formerly, partner in Brown Brothers Harriman & Co.; served as Special Assistant to the Secretary of War (1940-1941) and as Assistant Secretary of War for Air (1941-1945). Now, Under Secretary of State.

JOSEPH E. McLEAN. Formerly, Secretary of the Committee on Public Administration, Social Science Research Council. Author of *William Rufus Day.* Now Lecturer in Politics, Princeton University and Research Associate, Princeton Surveys.

DONALD C. STONE. Formerly, executive director of the Public Administration Service; lecturer, Syracuse University; formerly Assistant Director in charge of Administrative

Management, U.S. Bureau of the Budget. Now, Director of Administration, Economic Cooperation Administration.

E. L. WOODWARD. Author of *War and Peace in Europe, 1815-1870, The Age of Reform,* and other historical works. Official editor of Documents on British Foreign Policy, 1919-1939. Now Professor of Modern History in the University of Oxford.

GPSR Authorized Representative: Easy Access System Europe - Mustamäe tee
50, 10621 Tallinn, Estonia, gpsr.requests@easproject.com